Holidays & Holy Days

Holidays & Holy Days

*Origins, Customs, and Insights on
Celebrations Through the Year*

SUSAN E. RICHARDSON

WITHDRAWN

SERVANT PUBLICATIONS
ANN ARBOR, MICHIGAN

Vine Books is an imprint of Servant Publications especially designed to
serve evangelical Christians.

Published by Servant Publications
P.O. Box 8617
Ann Arbor, Michigan 48107

Cover design by Alan Furst, Inc. - Minneapolis, MN

01 02 03 04 10 9 8 7 6 5 4 3 2 1

Printed in the United States of America
ISBN 1-56955-306-8

Library of Congress Cataloging-in-Publication Data

Richardson, Susan E.
    Holidays and holy days : origins, customs, and perspectives on
celebrations through the year / Susan E. Richardson.
        p. cm.
    Includes bibliographical references.
    ISBN 1-56955-306-8 (acid-free)
     1. Fasts and feasts—History. 2. Holidays. 3. Church year. I. Title.

BV43 .R49 2001
263'.9—dc21

2001033157

To my mother, Martha Richardson,
for all those trips to the library when I was growing up,
and,
to my father, Marvin Richardson,
for teaching me that when you want to know something,
look it up.

Contents

Before We Begin

The book you're holding is one I wished for many times over the years as I worked in a Christian bookstore. Customers came in asking about holiday customs or how a holiday got started, and I had nothing in stock that would answer their questions. That is where this book comes in—I wrote it to answer those questions as well as I could.

During my research, I discovered that many questions don't have a specific answer. Christians have been arguing about what holidays—if any—should be celebrated and how to celebrate them since Christianity began.

For example, in A.D. 245, an early church leader, Origen, wrote that even contemplating celebrating Jesus' birthday was a sin. Christians in Armenia and Syria accused Roman Christians of sun worship for celebrating Christmas on December twenty-fifth.

During the fourth century, Augustine of Hippo stated, "we hold this day holy, not like the pagans because of the birth of the sun, but because of him who made it." Then Pope Gregory I sent Augustine of Canterbury to England in A.D. 596 as a missionary, instructing him to observe the people's customs, giving old traditions Christian meaning to help spread the faith, for "it is impossible to cut off everything at once."

The discussion still goes on today. You may believe that Christians should abandon customs with roots in pre-Christian celebrations. On the other hand, you may believe that the current meaning of the custom is important, not the origin.

I don't plan to take sides in this or any argument. As these different pre-Christian celebrations come into the text, along with church decrees for and against various traditions, I'll present them without drawing any conclusions. What the origins of our customs mean to Christian holiday celebrations is—I believe—for you as an individual believer to decide.

No one can write a book like this without a lot of help. Without the encouragement, suggestions, and support of Angie Hunt this book might never have gone from a dream into reality. Angie, I know I've said it before, but I'll say it again: thank you!

Terri Blackstock has my profound gratitude for her prayers, support, and friendship over the years, not just during this process.

Pamela Brown and Ann Jacobson, my readers, have my appreciation for plowing through an early draft, giving me suggestions and comments on the content, then still being willing to look at an extra chapter.

Kay Emery, recently retired from DaySpring Cards, and Jim Hauskey of DaySpring Cards made my section on Clergy Appreciation Day possible by putting me in touch with others, sending me information, and offering suggestions on that section. Jerry Frear of Under His Wing and Dan Davidson of Focus on the Family provided the remaining information on Clergy Appreciation Day.

Thanks, too, to Deborah Keener of the Wayne County Public Library for responding to an e-mail request for help, then moving my query to the top of the stack when my schedule moved up.

And finally, in the words of Paul: "Thanks be to God for his indescribable gift!" (2 Cor 9:15).

Holidays and Holy Days

Holiday celebrations have existed as long as humans have. Over the years, people have celebrated seasons, life changes, and divine beings. Maybe we have a God-given need to mark special days and events. After all, God used celebrations and feasts to mark special days for the Jewish people. He also designed them to foreshadow Jesus' coming.

We get the word *holiday* from a blend of *holy day*. Early in history, all holidays were holy days, whether Christian or pagan. Christianity wasn't born into a vacuum. Our faith came into a world where customs already existed.

Jewish customs provided the foundation for Christianity. Jesus was born into a Jewish family and lived a traditional Jewish life throughout His earthly ministry. Scripture tells us that He observed the feasts and holy days of Judaism. Not only did He attend worship in synagogues, He did some of His teaching there.

Since God designed the Jewish celebrations to point to Jesus as Messiah, Jewish customs and holy days were a natural part of newer Christian celebrations. Most of the first Christians were Jews. This quickly changed as Christianity grew.

Jesus had commanded that Christianity not be restricted to Jews. The apostles went beyond the Jewish community to win converts. Wherever they went, new Christians came to faith with a pre-existing set of ideas and customs.

Church history tells us that the early Christians opposed anything contrary to the gospel. Many people chose to die rather than worship the emperors of Rome as gods. If they saw a custom as pagan, they refused to take part in it.

They saw other customs as harmless or immediately gave them new meanings. Sometimes, old customs became a part of Christian worship when the former pagan beliefs no longer seemed to be a threat.

Thanks to the roads provided by the Roman Empire, missionary efforts spread further across the globe. Each new culture added more customs. The church sanctioned some additions. Others customs weren't sanctioned, but simply refused to die out.

In America, immigrants from around the world settled in the new country, bringing together a variety of customs and traditions for the first time. As America grew and changed, ethnic groups traded different traditions. English, Scotch, Irish, German, and other national backgrounds lived in a common land with a new common identity as Americans.

As a result, holiday celebrations in America became multicultural affairs. Along the way, they have also changed from holy days to holidays. Some holidays aren't tied in to religious tradition. Others may have begun as religious observances but now have added different elements from other sources.

This leaves the modern Christian with many questions. Why do we do the things we do? Which parts are from Christian tradition and which from other sources? The profile of each holiday or holy day will try to answer these questions.

Church History—A Brief Glimpse

As you look at many holidays, you'll find many began in the "Eastern church" or the "Western church". These may make more sense if we start with a brief look at how the early church grew.

You can find much of the early history in the Book of Acts. After the portions of history recorded in Scripture, centers of faith grew in several places. Gradually, people referred to these centers by location: in the East or in the West.

For the first part of Christian history, Jerusalem was the center of the church. From there, the apostles first went out to spread the gospel. Other Eastern centers of the church grew from Jerusalem. People in Antioch first called the followers of Jesus *Christians*. Antioch became a center for the young church. Other centers grew in Alexandria (Egypt); Byzantium—otherwise known as Constantinople—and Istanbul (modern Turkey).

Since these centers were close to where Christianity began, many early observances of Christian holy days can be traced to the Eastern church. Over time, the gradual rise of Roman Catholicism made the Western church important in setting celebrations. Catholic missionaries in Europe and America won many converts. When Rome accepted a holy day, all Catholics immediately accepted it, too. The more people who looked to Rome for leadership, the more Rome set what holy days people observed.

Other parts of the West shared leadership with Rome. Centers in Carthage (North Africa); Toledo (Spain); and Tours (in western Europe) influenced church direction. Monasteries in Britain and Ireland grew in influence as well. All of these added to traditions accepted by the Western church.

Unfortunately, East and West often disagreed over what holy days should be celebrated and when they should be celebrated. Even today, you'll find differences remaining between the two. We'll look only at the historical differences.

Beyond the division between the East and the West, another breach occurred in the sixteenth century: the Protestant Reformation. As with the previous division, the Reformation changed both customs and holy days. Since the Reformation will come up later, here are a few basics to help you.

If you know a little about church history already, you probably think of Martin Luther when you think of the Protestant Reformation. He is, undoubtedly, the best known of the Reformers, but he wasn't alone. At the same time that Luther was writing in Germany, other men were also calling for reforms within the Catholic church.

Luther's idea of reformation had nothing to do with forming a new denomination. He wrote against the practice of selling indulgences. The Lutheran church today takes its name from those who followed his interpretation of Scripture.

Because Luther was conservative in his reforms, the Lutheran church services looked much like Catholic services. He simplified the liturgy and included new music, but the biggest change was that Lutheran pastors preached a different theology. They emphasized personal redemption through grace rather than a works-based salvation.

Few customs, or normally observed holy days, changed. Luther discouraged the idea of praying to the saints and observing saints' days. Beyond that, the Lutheran church still celebrated the same holy days as the Catholic church did.

About the same time Luther was writing about the need for reformation in Germany, Huldrych Zwingli was preaching reformation in nearby Switzerland. The two differed in their focus. While Luther was concerned with purifying the church from its excesses, Zwingli believed that any forms of worship not specifically mentioned in Scripture were in error.

Zwingli's leadership resulted in a drastic change in worship. His followers removed all paintings, pictures, and statues from churches. They abandoned the old liturgy and holy days, and replaced hymns with psalms. Services in the resulting Reformed churches looked different from the older forms of worship.

Similar reforms took place elsewhere, with the result that some holy day celebrations mentioned later might not be familiar to you if you belong to a non-liturgical church. If Scripture did not specifically mention holy days, reformers discarded them along with other parts of Catholic worship.

The English Reformation took place over a longer period of time. It began when King Henry VIII took over the leadership of the English church from the Pope. Later Edward VI continued the reform along the lines of the Swiss Reformation.

When Elizabeth I came to the throne, she was a Protestant. Her tolerance allowed groups like the Puritans to practice their more austere style of Christianity. The growth of the Puritans, in turn, led to the English Civil War in the seventeenth century and the Commonwealth years under the rule of Oliver Cromwell, a Puritan.

As with other reforms, the changes in England affected various customs and holy day celebrations that appear later. The Church of England (Anglican Church) remained liturgical, following the basic liturgical year, while other denominations abandoned the liturgy along with other practices.

The history of your own denomination explains why some customs may or may not be familiar to you. We all inherit the decisions about customs made by those who came before us in faith.

Telling Time

You might think that New Year's Eve and New Year's Day are the logical holidays with which to begin. However, before we can look at how we celebrate the New Year, let's look at a "year" and the origin of the word "calendar".

For most of history, people celebrated the coming of a new year at the vernal equinox, the time in spring when day and night are of equal length. People usually celebrated this on March 25, though the actual date can vary somewhat.

So who came up with the idea of January 1 starting the new year? The Romans first used January 1 as New Year's Day in 153 B.C., but they didn't start a new calendar then. The date they used for the New Year varied until Julius Caesar officially reformed the calendar much later in 45 B.C.

He based the new calendar on the Egyptian calendar with a few changes. The Egyptians had thirty days in all of their months with five days left to complete the year. They added these days on at the end of the year as a festival before the new year began.

Caesar changed this method. He spread the extra five days throughout the year. Most months still had only thirty days, but some had thirty-one. The Julian calendar also established leap year every four years, though people didn't use the term until later. As a reward for Caesar's work, the Roman senate renamed his birth month, Quintilis, *July* in his honor.

As you might imagine, trying to change the entire calendar resulted in a lot of chaos. Caesar lengthened and manipulated the year so the seasons would match the months on January 1 of the following year.

The calendar change created a few other problems as well. The names September, October, November, and December simply mean the seventh, eighth, ninth, and tenth months. When the calendar changed, so that the new year began on January 1 instead of March 25, the names no longer fit.

For a time succeeding emperors gave these months new names. People found the constant changes as confusing as the wrong names. Eventually the old, though incorrect, names outlived all the others and stuck.

Despite Caesar's efforts, after the fall of the Roman Empire and the rise of Christian nations in Europe, most countries returned to considering March 25 as New Year's Day. Then, in 1582, Pope Gregory XIII made the reforms that established our present day method of calculating and dividing the year. At his proclamation, Catholics in Europe immediately adopted the revised calendar.

Protestants in Europe, however, were in the midst of the Reformation, when people viewed with suspicion anything vaguely connected with the Pope. As a result, acceptance of the new Gregorian calendar took longer. The Protestant portions of Germany finally adopted it in 1700—almost one hundred years after the Catholics accepted it. It took another fifty years before Great Britain, including the American colonies, did so in 1752.

Other parts of the world, such as the Asian countries, considered it the "Christian calendar," but eventually adopted it as well. Japan began using the new calendar in 1873, and China in 1912. Russia actually adopted it twice, first in 1918, then again in 1940 after trying various other calendars.

The Gregorian calendar came to America before Great Britain adopted it. The Dutch settlers, as well as Swedes and other European immigrants, already used the Gregorian calendar. In New England some groups such as the Quakers used the calendar, but renamed the months and days to remove pagan associations. They simply called each one "First Month" or "First Day."

The Roman word *kalends* or *calends* became our modern word *calendar*. To the Romans the word meant the first day of the month and the new moon, since the two originally coincided.

The Christian custom of measuring years from the birth of Christ didn't begin until almost A.D. 550. A Roman monk named Dionysius Exiguus worked out the new method. All of the older dates mentioned have been changed to agree with current calendar dating.

Weeks. We're so used to the seven-day week that you may find it hard to think of other possibilities. The Egyptians had ten days in their weeks, while the Assyrian week was six days long. Before they changed the calendar, the Roman week had eight days.

We get our seven-day week from two different sources. The Babylonians thought the moon took seven days for each of its four phases. Their calendar based a month on the moon's cycle, so dividing the month into four seven-day week cycles made sense.

The other source for the seven-day week is the Bible and Jewish tradition. God created the earth in seven days, setting the pattern for us to follow.

The names of the days of the week come from Old English. Tuesday, Wednesday, Thursday, and Friday come from Saxon gods or goddesses. Sunday, Monday, and Saturday come from a Babylonian idea that a different planet ruled each day. They considered the sun and moon to be planets also, so they included the sun's day and the moon's day, too.

Birthstones

Birthstones appear on nearly everything, not just jewelry. If you've ever wondered about the flower and gemstone for each month, you'll find them listed on each month's page.

Supposedly, each birthstone brings both powers and virtues or misfortune to influence a person.

The idea of a specific stone belonging to a particular month has been around for centuries. Some say the idea began with the twelve stones in the High Priest's breastplate, as mentioned in the Old Testament. Later they were linked with the twelve signs of the zodiac. Now they are used more out of custom.

The modern list of stones has more to do with business sense than with superstition. In 1912, the American National Retail Jewelers' Association adopted the current list of stones at its convention.

Sunday Worship

The Jewish people originally set aside Saturday—the Sabbath—for worship, and Saturday worship was familiar to the early believers.

In the earliest days of Christianity, the apostles went to the temple regularly, where they preached the good news of Jesus. Their early missionary work focused on preaching in the synagogues.

The Bible doesn't tell us if they kept the holy days of the Jewish faith. Because they spent so much time in the temple, it makes sense that they probably did so. The fact that they were all together on Pentecost—an important holy day— shows they probably still celebrated them.

Since Jesus rose on a Sunday, the early believers thought it an obvious choice for Christian worship. Early in Christianity, believers met on the first day of the week. Soon, they began to call this "the Lord's Day."

Many Jewish believers still kept the Sabbath, while also commemorating Sunday as the day of Christ's resurrection. They never questioned remembering Jesus' resurrection and worshipping on Sunday. As time went on the question for Jewish believers became whether to keep the Sabbath as well.

As the number of believers grew, two things began to happen that would eventually change how Christians worshipped. First, the church came under persecution by the Jewish establishment. This forced believers out of the synagogues and often into hiding. Second, the church grew beyond the Jewish community, as Gentiles became believers in Jesus.

These Gentiles had no background in the Jewish faith, so one of the first problems was whether Gentiles had to follow Jewish customs. You can read the discussion found in Acts 15. Throughout the New Testament, there are other hints of disagreement between Jewish Christians and Gentile Christians as the two groups struggled to understand just what their common faith meant.

While Sunday worship was universal, keeping the Sabbath varied from group to group until near the end of the second century, when there was an increase of interest in the Sabbath among Gentile Christians.

Many churches continued to celebrate both the Sabbath and Sunday until around A.D. 360, when the Council of Laodicea forbade keeping both. Even before that, the focus had begun to shift from the Sabbath to Sunday. With Sunday accepted as the day for Christian worship, only the form of worship and customs surrounding Sunday remained to be decided.

Time of Early Worship

Some authorities believe that the early Christians' form of worship grew out of the Jewish Sabbath worship. The Sabbath ran from sunset on Friday through sunset on Saturday. By waiting until after sunset, believers could move from the Sabbath to the following Lord's Day easily. Doing so allowed Jewish traditions and Christian worship to blend. The Sabbath ends with a special blessing over a cup of wine. For Jewish believers, including their new faith in the traditional prayers of thanksgiving and praise probably made sense, adding the distribution of bread and wine as Christ commanded.

Another source denies this possibility, stating that any evening worship held by early Christians was on Sunday evening, not the previous Saturday evening. In this case, the days would have to be measured according to Roman tradition, which, like our own, held that days ran from midnight to midnight.

Though most early believers were Jewish, Gentile believers quickly became part of the church, so both possibilities may be correct. Jewish believers may have held to their time measurement and blended the two celebrations while Gentiles met at a different time, still on the Lord's Day.

Form of Early Worship

Today's worship service looks much like that of the early believers. Justin, writing before A.D. 165, explains that worship began with a reading of the memories of the apostles or the prophets. Once the reading had finished, the day's leader spoke, urging the congregation to listen and apply what they had heard. They followed with prayer before bringing bread and wine. Deacons distributed the bread and wine to worshippers. After the services, deacons also took portions to absent members.

After the believers celebrated the Lord's Supper, they took an offering. The leader took charge of the money to be distributed to any in need. The church took particular care of orphans and widows, but anyone in need received a portion.

Part of this form is similar to Jewish synagogue services. Reading from the Old Testament and then an explanation of the passage was a major part of Jewish worship. This moved into the early church with readings from the apostles or letters from church leaders added to the Old Testament readings.

Other traditions in our current worship also spring from the earliest days of Christianity. In many churches you may stand when the Gospel is read. This goes back to early worship, when worshippers stood for the entire service. At this time, standing was an expression of respect and reverence. This carried over into modern worship as a sign of respect for the Gospel.

At the same time when standing was common in worship, people thought of kneeling as a position of servitude and slavery. Therefore, kneeling wasn't a common part of worship. Gradually people began to think of kneeling with penance or supplication. When they prayed for forgiveness or asked for specific things, they knelt. Kneeling for communion became popular later as the focus shifted to Christ's divinity and man's unworthiness.

People stood for services for hundreds of years. The Reformation spread the popularity of pews in the sixteenth century. Pastors began to spend more time teaching and preaching. As the services grew longer, people needed to sit so they could concentrate on the message.

The idea behind wearing good clothes on Sunday actually predates Christianity. Both ancient Romans and Jews dressed in their best to worship.

Sunday as a Day of Rest

On March 3, 321, Emperor Constantine forbade unnecessary work on Sunday. His declaration may not have been entirely to support the Christian faith. Sun worship was also part of his empire, and setting aside Sunday allowed both Christians and sun worshippers to gather for worship more easily.

His decree made it easier for Christians to practice their faith. He also allowed Christian soldiers to be excused from duty to attend services.

The early church interpreted the commandment to "remember the Sabbath day by keeping it holy" to refer to any sinful activity on the Lord's Day. After Constantine, the idea of Sunday as a day of rest continued to grow. Some believers thought that if the Jews observed the Sabbath by not working, then Christians should observe Sunday even more strictly because the new covenant of Christ surpassed the old covenant of the Law.

The church began calling for the discipline of anyone who worked on Sunday. The Council of Nabonne in A.D. 589 recommended severe punishment including whipping for those breaking Sunday rest. Then in A.D. 789 Emperor Charlemagne ruled that any work on Sunday was a violation of the Ten Commandments and this prohibition eventually passed into church law.

Today we still have a mixed group of ideas and laws regarding working on Sunday. In the early years of America, any kind of work on Sunday was forbidden. Laws frequently upheld the common custom. Over the years, the laws have changed. Now many people go shopping on Sunday just as they would any other day of the week. Christians must decide individually how they will keep Sunday as a day of worship and rest, since the government no longer decides it for us.

January

Let January's maiden be
all Garnet gemmed with constancy. *

Birthstone: Garnet
Birthstone Virtue: Constancy and faithfulness
Flower: Carnation

January was named for the Roman god, Janus, who was often shown with two faces looking opposite directions; he was the god of beginnings and endings. This made him a logical choice for the first month of the year, once the calendar changed.

* The couplets under each month comprise a larger traditional poem. See Willard A. Heaps, *Birthstones* (New York: Meredith Press, 1969).

New Year's Celebrations
January 1

Because people associated the coming of a new year with change, throughout history they believed that this was a perilous time when evil had more power. Our modern celebrations hold pieces of different rituals designed to help people pass safely through this dangerous time.

The first part of early New Year's rituals was to deal with the end of the old year. Everything old needed to be thrown out to make way for the new. Fasts or other kinds of deprivation "used up" the last of the old year, and served as a form of cleansing to prepare for the New Year. If you attend your church's watch night services, you may be following the same pattern today. Going to church on New Year's Eve allows people to begin the New Year in meditation with a focus on God.

The next step in older rituals was to get rid of evil, both personally and as a community. People removed personal evil by confessing sins, while taking care of the community by driving out demons. Many cultures utilized masked processions as part of New Year's celebrations. In this case, the masks usually represented the souls of the dead. The traditions might include a banquet or ceremony to welcome the dead. In the end, processions led the dead away from the living.

People also used noise to frighten evil away. Although firecrackers are the major modern day method of noisemaking, you may also hear church bells, drums, car horns, sirens, boat whistles, or party horns. Today's noise is just for fun—not to frighten demons—but it goes back directly to ancient New Year's celebrations.

Once the old year had ended and evil had been removed,

people needed to start the new year right. In some cultures they put out old fires before the end of the old year and then built new ones when the New Year began. Everything old ended with the old fire being extinguished and started fresh with the new one being lit.

Some people staged fights between two opposing teams representing good and evil. In this case, they believed that good must win over evil to guarantee a good year. If you spend New Year's Day watching ball games on television, you could blame them on this old custom. Someone from an older culture would feel right at home watching the games.

Once the community had successfully started the new year, they celebrated. Some chose feasts while others drank or engaged in other kinds of excesses. Today's drinking on New Year's Eve has its roots in older celebrations of successfully completing a difficult time. Excessive drinking may also be the remainder of an earlier custom that re-enacted on a personal level the chaos that existed before God brought order into the cosmos.

A familiar symbol of New Year's Day, the Baby New Year made its first modern appearance in a fourteenth century German folk song. Even before then people had called the new year "the newborn one." The actual custom has deeper roots, going back to ancient Greece and the festival of Dionysus. During this festival, revelers paraded a baby cradled in a winnowing basket to symbolize the rebirth of Dionysus as the spirit of fertility.

Epiphany
January 6

What was the first holy day celebrated by Christians? Not a Jewish holy day celebrated before Jesus' coming or even one celebrated in conjunction with His ministry. If you answered Christmas or even Easter, you would be wrong, though the Resurrection itself was celebrated before the Church established a fixed holy day.

Clement of Alexandria, Egypt, first mentioned Epiphany as a celebration at the end of the second century. The date—January 6—may have been chosen to compete with pagan feasts. At least two such celebrations were held on that date. Egyptians celebrated the winter solstice and honored their sun god on January sixth. Alexandrians honored the birth of their god, Acon, on January fifth.

We get the word *epiphany* from the Greek *epiphaneia.* Among the ancient Greeks, an epiphany was the appearance of a god or supernatural being. It was also a festival that commemorated such a visitation at a definite place. Christians celebrate three different events in Jesus' life at Epiphany. Each event revealed Christ to us in a different way.

First, the visit of the Magi to Jesus as a child revealed him as God of the Gentiles. Second, his baptism by John illustrated his divinity. Third, the miracle of water into wine at the wedding in Cana proved his divine power.

Eastern churches focus more on Jesus' baptism during Epiphany. In most Western churches—both Catholic and Protestant—you will see the visit of the Magi emphasized. Since Epiphany follows closely after Christmas, this fits into the general holiday season.

The twelve days from Christmas to Epiphany form the liturgical celebration of Christmas. Most scholars believe the Magi visited some time after the birth, rather than being at the manger, making the interval between the celebration of Jesus' birth and the arrival of the Magi appropriate.

From the visit of the Magi, celebrated at Epiphany, come two other customs: the king cake and gift giving at Christmas. The king cake first appears as part of Epiphany at the end of the fourteenth century. Though people baked the cake in celebration of the Magi's visit, they also chose a "king" for the day. The cook added a coin, bean, or other object to the cake. The person who got the slice with the token became "king" of the celebration. This custom moved into modern Mardi Gras celebrations and isn't associated with Epiphany now.

Originally, Christian leaders forbade giving gifts at Christmas because of the pagan associations with the tradition. Romans of all ranks commonly exchanged gifts called *strenae* at New Year's celebrations. Believers originally celebrated Jesus' birth on January sixth. The date being close to New Year's Day led to a variety of Roman New Year's customs, including gift giving, merging with Christmas celebrations.

So closely was the idea of gift giving tied to paganism that early Christians resisted the idea. Over time, though, Christian celebrations began including gift giving, with the explanation that gifts commemorated the Magi's gifts to Jesus. In fact, today that is the explanation you will be most likely to hear for why we give Christmas presents, without any mention of the fact that gift giving was once forbidden in Christian practice.

February

In fitful February it's a verity
the amethyst denotes sincerity.

Birthstone: Amethyst
Birthstone Virtue: Prevention of violent passions
Flower: Violet

The Romans held special ceremonies of repentance on the fifteenth of this month. In Latin, *februare* means "to purify."

Candlemas
February 2

Candlemas commemorates Jesus' presentation at the temple and Mary's purification as required under Jewish law (see Lev 12:6-8). After Jesus' birth, Mary and Joseph took him to the temple to fulfill the Law. There the Holy Spirit directed Simeon to them. Luke's Gospel describes him as "righteous and devout," one who was waiting for the promised Messiah. Simeon took Jesus in his arms and praised God, declaring that he had now seen the long awaited Savior.

Simeon's declaration of Jesus' identity became the focus for Candlemas. About A.D. 390, a nun from northwestern Spain, Etheria, gave the first historical description. She provides the first known information about many early church customs. Here she tells of the celebration in Jerusalem beginning with a solemn procession in the morning, followed by a sermon on the gospel text and ending with a mass.

During Etheria's time, believers celebrated Candlemas on February fourteenth. The early Christians originally celebrated Jesus' birth at Epiphany on January sixth. Since Jesus' presentation was forty days after his birth, they simply called the day *Quadragesima de Epiphania* ("fortieth day after Epiphany"). When leaders later agreed on December 25 for Christmas, the date for Candlemas moved to February second.

Some scholars believe that church leaders introduced Candlemas to counteract the Roman Lupercalia, because the early date of February 14 was close to Lupercalia on February fifteenth. A part of this celebration was a Feast of Purification connected with the goddess Ceres.

Other scholars claim there is no historical link with

Lupercalia, since the festival of Mary's purification was never held on February 14 in the Western church. When a candle-light procession became a part of the Candlemas celebration in the seventh century, people hadn't celebrated Lupercalia for three hundred years.

The Eastern church celebrated Candlemas before Rome adopted it. In A.D. 542, Emperor Justinian ordered a celebration in Constantinople in thanksgiving for the end of plague in the city. From there, the celebration spread throughout the East.

Rome adopted Candlemas for the Western church in the seventh century. They gave it the name *Hypapante* or "the meeting," referring to Simeon meeting Jesus outside the temple. At the same time, Pope Sergius I introduced the procession still a part of celebrations in the Catholic church.

Churches that celebrate Candlemas still bless the candles used during the year. The candles point to Simeon's statement that Jesus was "a light for revelation to the Gentiles." This part of Candlemas began in the eighth century and became common by the eleventh century. It was popular in England, from which we get the name Candlemas or "candle mass."

Despite the pre-Christian traditions, the Church intended candles used at Candlemas to have Christian symbolism. After the priest blesses and distributes them to the congregation, worshippers light them while they sing the *Nunc Dimittis*—Simeon's prayer. They carry the candles around the church reminding us of the True Light of Christ entering into the world.

At one time, the Christmas season traditionally ended at Candlemas. People took down all decorations and stored them for the next year. They burned the Christmas greenery and spread the ashes over the fields to insure a good growing season.

Groundhog Day
February 2

Have you ever wondered about the groundhog? Or maybe you just got confused about what the shadow is supposed to mean. The idea that a groundhog and his shadow on February 2 tells us something about the weather seems to be a blend of two traditions brought to America.

Primarily it comes from a medieval belief that various hibernating animals come to the surface on Candlemas morning, also celebrated on February 2, to observe the weather. In some places the hedgehog was the animal that foretold the weather. In Germany, forecasts were the badger's responsibility. Immigrants to America transferred its abilities to the groundhog or woodchuck.

In England and Scotland, the weather on Candlemas determined future weather. If Candlemas was fair, then more winter was expected. If overcast, then winter was over. When people blended this idea with the groundhog, it became the belief that if the groundhog saw his shadow, there would be six more weeks of winter.

No one has been able to find out why the weather at Candlemas should have anything to do with future weather.

The earliest known reference to Groundhog Day is an entry in James L. Morris' diary dated February 4, 1841. His entry also verifies the German origin of the custom. He wrote: "Last Tuesday, the 2nd was Candlemas day, the day on which, according to the Germans, the Groundhog peeps out of his winter quarters and if he sees his shadow he pops back for another six weeks nap, but if the day be cloudy he remains out, as the weather is to be moderate."

Valentine's Day
February 14

Why a day dedicated to two or more Christian martyrs named Valentine came to be associated with lovers is a mystery, although there are several theories.

Early lists of church martyrs show at least three men named Valentine. All have their feast day on February fourteenth. The first man was simply listed in a group of martyred believers. Of the other two, one was a priest and the other was the bishop of Interamna. Emperor Claudius II reportedly had both men beaten and beheaded in A.D. 269. These pieces of information gradually blended into a single figure.

You can find a number of legends about Valentine. One tells that while imprisoned, he cured the jailer's daughter of blindness. Another says that he fell in love with the jailer's daughter and sent her a letter signed "from your Valentine," thereby sending the first Valentine greeting.

Another story relating to his eventual patronage of lovers takes place during the reign of Emperor Claudius II. The Emperor wanted to recruit men as soldiers, but they didn't want to leave their wives and sweethearts. Furious, the Emperor forbade marriages and canceled all engagements. Valentine, however, was sympathetic to young lovers and married several couples in secret. When the Emperor discovered what Valentine had done, he had him thrown in prison.

More than likely, Valentine's Day is a Christianized form of the ancient Roman feast of Lupercalia. During the celebration, young men drew young women's names from a box. The young man then became the woman's partner for the festival.

Early Christian clergy objected to the pagan celebration and substituted the names of saints. During the following year the young man then attempted to emulate the saint he had drawn. People celebrated Lupercalia one day after Valentine's Day and the two merged over the years.

Still another possible explanation comes from the Middle Ages in Europe. People believed that birds began to mate on February fourteenth. Chaucer preserved evidence of this belief in his *Parliment of Foules*. He states, "For this was Seynt Valentyne's day. When every foul cometh ther to choose his mate."

Credit for sending the first valentine goes to Charles, Duc d'Orleans. In 1415, while imprisoned in the Tower of London, he sent his wife valentine poems. Some point to this as the earliest evidence for the rhymed valentines popular throughout history. Others held that the Duke's letter was a one-time incident, not a tradition.

A 1477 English Valentine's Day letter is the oldest certain valentine in existence. This letter shows that people sent valentines not long after the poems sent by the Duc D'Orleans. It would seem to support the idea that his letter was representative of this custom instead of a unique occurrence. Margery Brews wrote to her fiancé John Paston and addressed him as "Right reverent and worshipful and my right well-beloved valentine." Later references to Valentine's Day can be found in Shakespeare, Drayton, and Pepys.

By the seventeenth century, the custom of sending valentine cards developed. People made their cards by hand, so the style depended entirely on the maker. The first commercial valentines came out around 1800. Cards varied from the elaborate, with lace and flowers, to the "penny dreadfuls" or inexpensive put-down cards. The name came from the fact that they cost only a penny, and the designs were dreadful.

In the United States, exchanging valentine cards probably

reached an all-time high during the Civil War. An 1863 periodical said of Valentine's Day "with the exception of Christmas, there is no festival throughout the year which is invested with half the interest belonging to this cherished anniversary."

In the first third of the twentieth century, the custom of sending valentines began to be observed by and for children. Remember "mailing" valentines for your classmates during your school days? The valentine "mailbox" where children could "mail" cards for their classmates became a common feature during this time.

Now you can buy valentines for every associate, from friends and family on down to business and casual acquaintances. From being a festival mainly for lovers, Valentine's Day has become a time to express appreciation and friendship on all levels.

Cupid. One of the most enduring symbols of Valentine's Day is Cupid. In Roman mythology, he was the god of love, taken from his Greek counterpart, Eros. According to most myths, Cupid was the son of Venus, Aphrodite in Greek, the goddess of love and beauty. In earlier stories writers described him simply as a slender youth.

The later better-known stories showed Cupid as a naked, winged boy carrying a bow and arrows. Cupid was often mischievous and frequently caused problems with his arrows. When he shot either humans or gods in the heart with the arrows, they fell in love.

During Hellenistic times, Eros (Cupid) went from being shown as merely one god to being multiplied into many "cupids" on frescos or ceramics. This representation has passed down to us today, though the cupid has also been Christianized as a baby angel.

Heart. In many early traditions, people once considered the heart to be the seat of emotions and affections. During the Middle Ages, people romanticized this idea and the stylized heart shape was born.

So how did we get the standardized heart shape? No one seems to be certain, though various possibilities have been raised. One source suggested that the heart is a stylized human buttock, or perhaps suggests a female torso. Another possibility is that is comes from the imprint of a kiss on paper. Regardless, the heart is now a universal symbol of love and affection.

Purim
Date varies - February/March

The basis of Purim is a celebration of Esther and Mordecai's victory over Haman. The modern Jewish observance includes reading the book of Esther, along with a festive family meal, sending gifts of food to friends, giving money for the poor, costumes, masquerades, plays, and heavy drinking.

The Book of Esther tells of a young Jewish girl named Hadassah. The Persian king, Xerxes, took her into his harem after the previous queen, Vashti, had been deposed. Hadassah was renamed Esther and became the new queen.

Meanwhile, outside the palace, her cousin Mordecai became embroiled in a power struggle with Haman, the king's Grand Vizier. When Mordecai refused to bow to Haman as the king had ordered, Haman created a plan to exterminate all Jews in the Persian Empire. Mordecai sent word to Esther, who agreed to go to King Xerxes. She succeeded in discrediting Haman, and the king executed him. Xerxes gave Mordecai Haman's former position, and saved the Jewish people from extermination.

Participants in modern Purim celebrations often bring noisemakers or stomp and hiss each time Haman's name is read. Others write Haman's name on the soles of their shoes and stamp until the name is erased.

Holding satiric plays and skits that poke fun at those usually held in reverence is another tradition. Celebrations in Israel include the injunction to drink until you can't tell the difference between cursed Haman and blessed Mordecai.

March

But oh, what shall a March maid do?
Wear a bloodstone and be firm and true.

Birthstone: Bloodstone, Aquamarine
Birthstone Virtue: Steadfast affection, courage, and wisdom
Flower: Jonquil

March was named for Mars, the Roman god of war.

St. Patrick's Day
March 17

Perhaps you shared a common problem on Saint Patrick's Day during your school years. Even if you weren't Catholic, you'd still probably heard about him and knew that you were supposed to wear green. If you forgot, you joined the other unfortunates in dodging pinches all day long or maybe arguing for the small bit of green in the pattern of your shirt.

Despite being one of the best-known saints, we know little for certain about St. Patrick. Though considered the patron saint of Ireland, he wasn't born there. In fact, we don't know his exact birthplace. In his book *Confession*, he gives his birthplace as Bannauem Taberniae, though no one now knows where the village was located.

Nor do we know if the date of his celebration, March 17, is his birth date or death date. Different sources make different claims. It may be neither. Various sources also give a variety of possible dates for his birth year. Possibilities range from A.D. 373, 386, 387, 389, to 395. He died either in 461 or around 492. Some legends say that he died at 120 years of age as Moses did. To add to the confusion, some scholars believe that there were two men named Patrick. Over the years people combined the stories about them into one man.

Patrick's original name was Maewyn. In his writings, he frequently spoke of himself as *patricius* or wellborn. This is where we get the English *Patrick*.

Patrick's own words are the best place for factual information. He opens his book, *Confession*, with a brief history of his life.

I, Patrick, a sinner, the most rustic and the least of all the faithful, and in the estimation of very many deemed contemptible, had for my father Calpornius, a deacon, the son of Potitus, a presbyter, who belonged to the village of Bannauem Taberniae; for close thereto he had a small villa, where I was made a captive.

"I was made a captive" refers to his capture at age sixteen by brigands, who took him to Ireland, and sold him into slavery. During this time, he became a Christian.

After six years as a slave, he had a vision in which he saw a ship that had been provided for his return to his family. He escaped on a boat carrying a cargo of Irish hounds to the continent. From there he returned home to his parents.

His return home was short-lived. Soon after returning, he had another vision, which he believed was a call from God to return to Ireland, this time as a missionary to share the good news of Christ with the Irish people.

He began preparing for his mission by going back to the European Continent from Britain. There he studied under the bishop of Auxerre, Germanus. In 432, he was ordained as bishop of Ireland and allowed to return.

The native Druid priests opposed his ministry. Patrick ignored their protests and continued with his work. Among other things, he began a tradition that continues to this day of lighting an Easter fire. At the time, he did so to counter the Druids' spring fire. He also caused consternation when he christened the Druids' fires, making them a symbol of Christ, the Light of the World.

By the end of his life, most people in Ireland had converted to Christianity. His followers finished the job within a few years after his death.

One of the more common stories about St. Patrick—how

he used a shamrock to explain the Trinity—may be authentic. He mentioned the Trinity often in his writings. Tradition claims he wrote the two hymns, "St. Patrick's Breastplate" and "The Deer's Cry," which both speak of the Trinity. He explained that the shamrock's three leaves represented the Father, the Son, and the Holy Spirit. A single stem representing the Godhead joined them. Just as the Father, the Son, and the Holy Spirit are all separate and yet are one God, the leaves of the shamrock are separate yet make up one plant.

In doing so, he chose to take a pagan symbol and gave it Christian meaning. He may have chosen to emphasize the Trinity because three was the number of the Druids' unknown god. The shamrock was an excellent way to make a difficult idea approachable to the people.

Another familiar story about Patrick is that he drove all the snakes out of Ireland. Some look at this literally—an Irish Pied Piper removing unwanted creatures. Others believe that this was a symbolic statement referring to the Druids, whose wisdom was often represented by a snake. St. Patrick drove the serpent of Druidic wisdom away, replacing their knowledge with the truth of Christ.

Today you may automatically think of the "wearin' of the green" when thinking of St. Patrick's Day, but the custom didn't begin until over one thousand years after St. Patrick's death. Another common custom's origins have proven elusive: the problem of getting pinched for forgetting to wear green on St. Patrick's Day. No sources mentioned how the custom began.

Mardi Gras
Date varies—February/March

If parades and trinkets come to mind when you hear Mardi Gras, you're not alone, but keep reading for the day's real meaning. The word *Mardi gras* literally means *fat Tuesday* (French). Strictly speaking, Mardi Gras is the Tuesday before the beginning of Lent, which starts on Ash Wednesday.

You can trace the name to the tradition of using up all eggs, milk, and fat in preparation for the forty days of Lent. During the Lenten fast, all of those products were prohibited. In the days before refrigeration, they would spoil before the fast was over. Since pancakes became a traditional way to use up these materials, people also called Mardi Gras "Pancake Day."

People in England called it Shrove Tuesday from the practice of confessing sins in preparation for Lent. *To shrive* means to confess and receive absolution.

The other side of Mardi Gras is carnival, the best-known being the yearly celebration in New Orleans. Many believe this aspect comes from a variety of pre-Christian fertility and spring rites, and various new year's customs. Early Egyptians, as well as Greeks and Romans, celebrated during this time of year.

Another source points out that there are five centuries between the last mention of pagan rites similar to carnival and the first medieval mention of the word. Lupercalia was last mentioned in A.D. 494 and *Carnelevare* was first mentioned in A.D. 965. The source suggests that carnival developed along with the church's rules about Lent, and the church may have fostered the pagan association to help suppress the festival's disorderliness.

The word carnival is from the Latin *carne vale* or "farewell meat." In this case, the meat refers to Lenten fasting, which begins the next day. At one time, carnival extended from Epiphany to Shrove Tuesday, though this isn't usually the case today.

Modern Mardi Gras came to America from France. In 1827, a group of students who had been studying in France came back to New Orleans and brought the custom with them. The first Mardi Gras featured a few masked participants in procession. From that beginning comes today's multi-parade extravaganzas.

The traditional colors for Mardi Gras are gold, green, and purple. One source interprets the colors as purple standing for royalty, gold for purity, and green for love and friendship. In the Rex parade of 1892, with the theme "Symbolism of Colors," the organization identified purple with justice, green with faith, and gold with power. Regardless, the colors provide a rich background for the celebrations.

The carnival aspects of Mardi Gras have nearly taken over the Christian ones. What was originally a day of preparation for Lent has now become an all-out extravaganza.

Ash Wednesday
Date varies—February/March

After Mardi Gras—the day, not the carnival season—comes Ash Wednesday and the beginning of Lent. Participants attending Ash Wednesday services receive the sign of the cross marked in ashes on their forehead. Frequently, the church saves the palms from the previous year's Palm Sunday celebration and burns them for use during Ash Wednesday services.

Originally, only "public sinners" received the ashes. Usually repentance was a private matter. In the case of a serious sin, the person who committed it had to make the sin public. Then he or she had to undergo a lengthy and difficult penance before being received back into the church. The term of penance lasted from Ash Wednesday to Holy Thursday—just before Easter—and involved many restrictions. Frequently, penitents were required to live in a monastery apart from others, performing manual labor. From this forty-day period of separation comes our word *quarantine*.

Though first intended only for public sinners, gradually other devout Christians began volunteering to receive ashes on this day. By the end of the eleventh century, the custom had become widespread rather than being restricted to notorious sinners.

Actually, Ash Wednesday is forty-six days before Easter, but forty days before Holy Week, which begins with Palm Sunday. Ash Wednesday was simply called "Beginning of the Fast" until 1099, when Pope Urban II gave it the current name.

Some have found the change from the party atmosphere to Ash Wednesday's repentance hard to understand. In 1592, Ogier Ghislain de Busbecq, an ambassador from Emperor

Ferdinand I to the court of Sultan Suleiman I, wrote a letter which told of a Turkish official who went to Europe on a diplomatic mission for the sultan and witnessed the carnival festivities prior to Lent. When he returned to Constantinople, he reported his observations to the sultan. According to his account, Christians went completely mad during a certain time of year, but when their priests sprinkled ashes on them, they immediately became sane. While this may have been a tall tale, Pope Benedict XIV took it seriously and quoted the account in his letter protesting the abuses of carnival celebrations.

In liturgical churches, the arrival of Lent includes the removal of the *alleluia* sung during services. *Alleluia* comes from Hebrew for "Praise the Lord." Church leaders considered it out of keeping with the sorrowful nature of Lent. In the early church, *alleluia* was only used at Easter, but later it spread to the rest of the year except for Lent. The *alleluia* returns to the church during the Mass of the Easter Vigil on the Saturday before Easter, foreshadowing the Resurrection.

Lent
Date varies – February/March/April

Our word Lent comes from the Anglo-Saxon *lencten*, meaning spring.Christians in Egypt established the traditional forty days of Lent before A.D. 330. Today people think of the forty days of Lent as remembering Jesus' forty days in the wilderness before He began His ministry. Forty shows up several places in Scripture. Moses spent forty days in the wilderness, the Jews wandered forty years before being allowed to enter the Promised Land, and Jonah gave Ninevah forty days to repent.

In the early church, new converts fasted for forty hours to prepare for baptism on Easter Eve. When Emperor Constantine made Christianity the official state religion of the Roman Empire in the fourth century, church leaders worried that the sudden increase in members would change the church's character. They tried to prevent this by requiring all Christians to participate in the Lenten fast, not just new converts.

Today most people think of fasting at Lent in terms of what they will give up. Fasting in the early days was a much more severe discipline. Pope Gregory defined fasting for the church at large in a letter to Saint Augustine in A.D. 604. "We abstain from flesh meat and from all things that come from flesh, as milk, cheese, eggs." The church considers Sundays a "little Easter" each week and exempts Sundays from fasting during Lent.

At least one Lenten food has been around since the Roman Empire. Christians used special dough consisting only of flour, salt, and water, conforming to the strictest possible fasting guidelines. They then shaped the dough like two arms crossed in prayer to remind them that Lent was a season of penance.

They called the bread *bracellae* or "little arms" in Latin. In German it became *brezel* or *prezel.* In English, of course, you know them as pretzels. Eating pretzels year-round became common during the nineteenth century, and their previous Lenten meaning was lost.

Another story of the pretzel comes much later. In this version, an Italian monk in A.D. 610 created pretzels when he used leftover bread dough to bake gifts for children who learned their prayers. He called them *pretiola* or "little reward." In this version, the twist still represents arms crossed in prayer, with the three holes representing the Trinity. Perhaps both are correct. The monk could easily have used the more austere Lenten pretzels as an idea and substituted bits of bread dough. Regardless of which story is correct, the pretzel originated from within the Church.

Draping the Cross. Many churches today drape an outdoor cross with fabric in liturgical colors to share the Easter season with the community. Inside, of course, the paraments on the altar and the clergy's vestments change color, too. Purple is the liturgical color of Lent and symbolizes penitence, so the first cloth is purple.

The purple cloth remains in place until Good Friday, when it is replaced with black, as a symbol of mourning for Jesus' crucifixion. The black cloth stays up until Easter Sunday when a white cloth replaces the black one. White symbolizes the great joy of the Resurrection.

A related custom shares the meaning of Easter with passersby. It starts the same as the draped cross, with a plain wooden cross in front of the church at the beginning of Lent. Some churches include a crown of thorns. On Easter Sunday morning, congregation members bring flowers from their homes to decorate the plain wood. The unadorned cross becomes a floral reminder of the new life Jesus' resurrection gives.

Palm Sunday
Date varies - March/April

With Palm Sunday, Lent ends and Holy Week begins. Throughout the week leading up to Easter Sunday, we remember and celebrate the events of Jesus' last week before the crucifixion. When Jesus rode into Jerusalem on a donkey, the people greeted Him with palm branches. At that time, a king rode to war on a horse. A king who came in peace, however, rode on a donkey.

Jesus proclaimed Himself to be the King of the Jews by choosing to ride a donkey into Jerusalem. Many recognized Him as the long-awaited Messiah, but some missed the symbolism of the donkey. They were still waiting for a warrior king to lead them against the Romans. Jesus came in peace to offer personal—not political—redemption.

Cyril, bishop of Jerusalem, instituted the Palm Sunday ritual between A.D. 382 and 386. For the Western church, the first reported observance is in Spain, probably in the fifth century. Oddly, the day wasn't celebrated in Rome before the twelfth century.

April

The April girl has a brave defense.
The diamond guards her innocence.

Birthstone: Diamond
Birthstone Virtue: Purity, repentance, and innocence
Flower: Sweetpea

The month's name is uncertain. It may come from a form of
Aphrodite, *Aprilis*, the goddess of love.

April Fool's Day
April 1

Like all children, you probably relished April Fool's Day. Being allowed to trick adults with far-fetched stories delights the child in all of us. In fact, a separate festival in India bears a striking resemblance to April Fool's Day, though most scholars feel that the similarity is a coincidence.

One favorite form of April fooling is sending someone on a fool's errand, such as asking for a biography of Adam's grandfather. One source suggested the origin of April Fool's Day involved such a fool's errand.

According to Roman mythology, the god of the underworld, Pluto, kidnapped Proserpine, the daughter of the goddess Ceres. Ceres heard her daughter's cries for help and began searching for her, as any mother would do. Most consider it a fool's errand because no one except Pluto could enter the underworld and return.

The most likely source for April Fool's Day is the calendar changeover in France. Before the change, people commonly celebrated the new year throughout the week following March twenty-fifth. Most French people exchanged visits and gave gifts on April 1, the last day of the new year's seven-day celebration or octave.

When Charles IX proclaimed January 1 as New Year's Day in 1564, the change took several years to be recognized. Part of the problem was poor communication, but more conservative members of society resisted the change. Those who embraced the new custom ridiculed the conservatives by making mock solemn visits on April 1 and sending gag gifts.

People in America knew about April Fool's Day before the calendar changeover took place here. Puritan Judge Sewall notes in his diary, "In the morning I dehorted Sam Hirst and Grindell Rawson from playing idle tricks because 'twas the first of April: They were the greatest fools that did so."

The English settlers apparently brought the custom of April Fool's Day to the New World with them.

Maundy Thursday
Date varies—March/April

Maundy Thursday commemorates the Last Supper, Jesus' agony in the Garden, and his arrest. The term *maundy* comes from the Latin *mandatum* (commandment), another tie to the Last Supper. Jesus' statement at the Last Supper, in Latin, is *Mandatum novum do vobis:* "A new commandment I give you" (Jn 13:34).

Church services today vary. Most will include the Lord's Supper. Some may include foot washing, too, just as Jesus washed His disciples' feet. Some churches have a tenebrae service. During worship, the altar candles are extinguished to show the temporary victory of darkness over light. Then parishioners may be asked to leave the sanctuary in silence to contemplate Jesus' sacrifice.

Good Friday
Date varies - March/April

Why we call the day of Jesus' crucifixion *good* has always been a mystery. Some sources suggest that *good* is a corruption of God's Friday. Others say that *good* simply refers to the good gift of salvation given on the cross. Other names for the day include Festival of the Crucifixion, Day of Salvation, Long Friday, and Holy Friday.

One of the oldest customs associated with Good Friday is eating hot cross buns. This custom may have had its origin in pre-Christian times. The Egyptians used small loaves stamped with symbolic horns in their worship of Isis. Greeks used cross-marked cakes associated with the goddess Diana. Archaeologists discovered two small loaves with crosses on them under the ruins of Herculaneum, which had been covered by volcanic ash after the eruption of Mt. Vesuvius in A.D. 79.

Early Christians celebrated with flat unleavened cakes similar to Passover loaves. Later the cakes were made with the same dough used to make the bread for communion. Hot cross buns are most popular in England, where tradition says they originated in 1361, when a monk at St. Alban's Abbey baked them to give to the poor. Just as with other customs, an older pagan tradition existed, but the modern one is many years removed from the earlier one.

Easter
Date varies—March/April

The early Christians began remembering the Resurrection every Sunday following its occurrence. In A.D. 325, the Council of Nicaea set aside a special day just to celebrate the Resurrection. The problem with an official day was deciding whether the Resurrection should be celebrated on a weekday or always on a Sunday.

Many felt that the date should continue to be based on the timing of the Resurrection during Passover. Once Jewish leaders determined the date of Passover each year, Christian leaders could set the date for Easter by figuring three days after Passover. Following this schedule would have meant that Easter would be a different day of the week each year, only falling on a Sunday once in awhile.

Others believed since the Lord rose on a Sunday and this day had been set aside as the Lord's Day, this was the only possible day to celebrate His resurrection. As Christianity drew away from Judaism, some were reluctant to base the Christian celebration on the Jewish calendar.

Finally the Council decided Easter should be celebrated on the Sunday following the first full moon after the vernal equinox. Since the date of the vernal equinox changed from year to year, calculating the proper date can be difficult. This is still the method used to determine Easter today, which is why some years we have Easter earlier than other years.

Since Easter is a celebration of Jesus' Resurrection, you would think there wouldn't be room for paganism. However, Easter is one of the holidays most intertwined with pagan symbolism and ritual.

The origin of the word *easter* isn't certain. The Venerable

Bede, an eighth-century monk and scholar, suggested that the word may have come from the Anglo-Saxon *Eostre* or *Eastre*— a Teutonic goddess of spring and fertility. Recent scholars haven't been able to find any reference to the goddess Bede mentioned and consider the theory discredited.

Another possibility is the Norse *eostur, eastur,* or *ostara,* which meant "the season of the growing sun" or "the season of new birth." The word *east* comes from the same roots. In this case, *easter* would be linked to the changing of the season.

A more recent and complex explanation comes from the Christian background of Easter rather than the pagan. The early Latin name for the week of Easter was *hebdomada alba* or "white week," while the Sunday after Easter day was called *dominica in albis* from the white robes of those who had been newly baptized. The word *alba* is Latin both for *white* and *dawn.* People speaking Old High German made a mistake in their translation and used a plural word for *dawn, ostarun,* instead of a plural for white. From *ostarun* we get the German *Ostern* and the English *Easter.*

Easter Bunny. What is the first thing that comes to mind when you think of Easter? As a Christian, the first image might be the cross or the empty tomb. For the general public, a blitz of media images and merchandise on store shelves makes it more likely that the Easter Bunny comes to mind. So how did a rabbit distributing eggs become a part of Easter?

There are several reasons for the rabbit, or hare, to be associated with Easter, all of which come through pagan celebrations or beliefs. The most obvious is the hare's fertility. Easter comes during spring and celebrates new life. The Christian meaning of new life through Christ and a general emphasis on new life are different, but the two gradually merged. Any animals—like the hare—that produced many offspring were easy to include.

The hare is also an ancient symbol for the moon. The date of Easter depends on the moon. This may have helped the hare to be absorbed into Easter celebrations.

The hare or rabbit's burrow helped the animal's adoption as part of Easter celebrations. Believers saw the rabbit coming out of its underground home as a symbol for Jesus coming out of the tomb. Perhaps this was another case of taking a pre-existing symbol and giving it Christian meaning.

Like many other customs, the modern Easter bunny seems to have a German origin. In a 1682 German book, the bunny lays eggs and hides them in the garden; even at this date it was referred to as an old fable. According to this account, the bunny laid red eggs on Maundy Thursday and other colors on Easter.

The Easter hare came to America with German immigrants, and the hare's role passed to the common American rabbit. Originally children made nests for the rabbit in hats, bonnets, or fancy paper boxes, rather than the baskets of today. Once the children finished their nests, they put them in a secluded spot to keep from frightening the shy rabbit. The appealing nests full of colored eggs probably helped the custom to spread.

Back in Southern Germany, the first pastry and candy Easter bunnies became popular at the beginning of the nineteenth century. This custom also crossed the Atlantic, and children still eat candy rabbits—particularly chocolate ones—at Easter.

Easter eggs. Next to the Easter bunny, the most familiar symbol is the Easter egg. Like others, the egg has a long pre-Christian history. Again there's no certainty as to why it became associated with Easter.

Many Ancient cultures viewed eggs as a symbol of life. Hindus, Egyptians, Persians, and Phoenicians believed the world began with an enormous egg. The Persians, Greeks, and Chinese gave gifts of eggs during spring festivals in celebration of new life all around them. Other sources say people ate dyed eggs at spring festivals in Egypt, Persia, Greece, and Rome. In ancient Druid lore, the eggs of serpents were sacred and stood for life.

Early Christians looked at the connection eggs had to life and decided eggs could be a part of their celebration of Christ's resurrection. In addition, in some areas, eggs were forbidden during Lent; therefore, they were a delicacy at Easter. Since many of the earlier customs were Eastern in origin, some speculate that early missionaries or knights of the Crusade may have been responsible for bringing the tradition to the West.

In the fourth century, people presented eggs in church to be blessed and sprinkled with holy water. By the twelfth century, the *Benedictio Ovorum* had been introduced, authorizing the special use of eggs on the holy days of Easter. The timing of this blessing would uphold the idea that Crusaders may have brought the tradition back. Even though eggs had been used previously, the Crusaders may have made the custom more popular and widespread.

In 1290, Edward I of England recorded a purchase of 450 eggs to be colored or covered with gold leaf. He then gave the eggs to members of the royal household.

Once the custom became accepted, new traditions began to grow up around it. Eggs were dyed red for joy, and in memory of Christ's blood. Egg rolling contests came to America from England, possibly as a reminder of the stone being rolled away.

What about the familiar Easter Egg hunt? One source suggested that it grew out of the tradition of German children searching for hidden pretzels during the Easter season. Since children were hiding nests for the Easter Bunny to fill with eggs at the same time they were hunting pretzels, it was only a small leap to begin hiding eggs instead.

Lamb. Of all Easter symbols, the lamb is probably the most strongly Christian. Other than the fact that lambs are young animals born in springtime, it has no strong ties to pagan traditions.

The lamb comes from the Jewish Passover, where each family killed a lamb as a sacrifice. When Christ became the Passover Lamb for everyone, the lamb became a symbol for His sacrifice on the cross.

New clothes at Easter. New clothes have long been associated with the idea of newness and a fresh beginning. The familiar custom of having new clothes for Easter probably began with early Christians wearing new white robes for baptism during Easter Vigil services. Later, the custom expanded to everyone wearing new clothes in celebration of his or her new life in Christ.

Sunrise services. The familiar sunrise service is a relatively new addition to Easter. A group of young Moravian men in Hernhut, Saxony held the first recorded sunrise service in 1732. They went to their cemetery called God's Acre at sunrise to worship in memory of the women who went to the tomb early on the first Easter morning and discovered it empty. Moravian immigrants brought the custom to America, with the first service in the United States held in 1743.

Easter lilies. The Easter lily is another new addition to Easter celebrations. Throughout the years, painters and sculptors used the white Madonna lily to symbolize purity and innocence, frequently referring to Mary. This lily doesn't force well, so nurseries couldn't get the flower to bloom in time for Easter.

In the 1880s, Mrs. Thomas Sargent brought Bermuda lily bulbs back to Philadelphia. A local nurseryman, William Harris, saw the lilies and introduced them to the trade. A more practical consideration was that they were easy to force into bloom in time for the Easter season. From there, the Bermuda lily, now the familiar Easter lily, spread throughout the country.

The Cross. The cross actually pre-dates Christianity. Egyptian and Babylonian monuments long before the time of Christ have crosses carved on them. In fact, early Christians rarely used the cross for the first two centuries following Jesus' death.

Later in the third century, Christians began to use disguised crosses such as the anchor cross, a ship with a mast, or the initials for Jesus and Christ in Greek or Latin superimposed to create a crosslike design.

After Constantine, the cross became an openly Christian symbol during the fourth century. Emperor Theodosius later abolished crucifixion and may have helped the symbolic cross become established as the immediate negative associations diminished.

The original cross may have been what is now known as a tau cross, a "T" shape. The word used in the Bible text doesn't give any clues to the exact appearance. The word simply means *tree* or *stake.* The most commonly used form is the Latin cross made of two plain pieces.

Via Dolorosa and the Stations of the Cross. Separating the two is difficult since the Via Dolorosa is the route Jesus may have followed on the way to the cross, and the stations of the cross commemorate the different events during the trip. The name for the route is Latin for "way of sorrows" or "way of suffering."

The tradition of commemorating the Stations of the Cross probably started when early pilgrims to Jerusalem followed the traditional route Jesus took from Pilate's house to Calvary. Pilgrims continued the practice through the crusades (1095-1270). After the crusades, Moslems recaptured Israel and pilgrimages were too dangerous.

During this time, various groups within the church built copies of the sepulcher that included markers to represent the events on the way to the cross. These allowed people to share in the experience of retracing Jesus' road to the cross without leaving the country and braving the political turmoil in the Middle East.

The Franciscans took the idea one step further during the Middle Ages. They put up wooden crosses in churches to represent the different events. The number of stations still varied, but there were usually about fourteen. Finally, in 1731, Pope Clement XII set the number of stations at the fourteen used today.

The stations are marked along the actual Via Dolorosa in Jerusalem. Many churches today still set up representations of the stations as devotional aids during Lent and Easter. Within the Catholic church, there is a strict set of rules as to how these should be presented.

The traditional Stations of the Cross are a mixture of factual events recorded in Scripture and legendary events added later. Those marked with an asterisk (*) are the events mentioned in Scripture.

1. Jesus is condemned to death. *
2. Jesus is made to carry His cross. *
3. Jesus falls under the weight of the cross for the first time.
4. Jesus meets Mary, His mother.
5. Simon of Cyrene is made to bear the cross. *
6. Veronica wipes Jesus' face.
7. Jesus falls the second time.
8. The women of Jerusalem weep for Jesus. *
9. Jesus falls the third time.
10. Jesus is stripped of his garments. *
11. Jesus is nailed to the cross. *
12. Jesus dies on the cross. *
13. Jesus is taken down from the cross. *
14. Jesus is placed in the tomb. *

At times a fifteenth station is added for the resurrection.

Veronica is one of the legendary additions, probably French in origin. The story tells that she offered Jesus her headcloth to wipe His face on His way to the cross. When He returned the veil, His features were imprinted on it.

The other additions, meeting His mother and falling under the cross, aren't specifically mentioned in the Scriptures. Scripture places Mary at the crucifixion, so an earlier meeting with her was certainly possible. Also, the fact that the Romans forced Simon of Cyrene to carry Jesus' cross makes it possible that He was so weak from the beating that He fell along the way.

Passover
Date varies—March/April

Like Easter, Passover is a holiday where the date is decided by the moon. Because of this, Passover may be celebrated before, during, or after Easter week. Though many people think of Passover as mainly a Jewish holiday, it is closely intertwined with Easter.

The Last Supper may have been a Passover meal. The Gospels of Matthew, Mark, and Luke indicate that the meal they shared was Passover, but the Gospel of John states that the meal was held on the Day of Preparation for the Passover. Many Christians now celebrate Passover in addition to Easter, recognizing Easter as completing the redemption fore-shadowed by offering the lamb at the first Passover.

In Exodus 12:1-20, God gave specific directions for the Passover feast, as well as directions for the accompanying Feast of Unleavened Bread. People often observed *passover* for the entire week that includes the Feast of Unleavened Bread, instead of just the single day of the Passover celebration.

The first Passover occurred when God released the people of Israel from their captivity in Egypt. As the last plague on the Egyptians, God put to death the firstborn of every household. God told the Israelites to kill a lamb and mark their doorways with its blood. When the Angel of Death came, it passed over the homes marked with blood.

Today there is no single way to celebrate Passover (or Pesah). How people celebrate depends on whether they are orthodox, conservative, or reform Jews. Even rabbinical tradition provides alternatives for parts of the celebration.

Celebrating Passover involves three major parts: telling the story of the Exodus, eating matzos (or unleavened bread), and refraining from either eating or owning *hametz* (anything made with leavening). These parts guide the celebration. The Seder meal provides a format for telling the story of the Exodus and eating matzos. Avoiding *hametz* takes place mainly during preparation.

Before Passover begins, all *hametz* must be removed from the home. Depending on how strict you are, this can include everything from a thorough cleaning to owning extra dishes for use only during Passover. On the day before Passover, people remove *hametz* from the home.

The main celebration of Passover focuses on the Seder meal and its accompanying Haggadah—a liturgy telling the Exodus story and providing the script for the evening. Foods on the Seder plate aren't actually eaten, but are the symbols needed for the celebration.

Three matzos are placed near the Seder plate. These may be stacked on top of each other or put in a special matzos cover with three compartments. During the celebration, everyone is required to drink four cups of wine, though substituting grape juice is allowed. Other requirements are salt water to symbolize tears and Elijah's cup, set aside for the prophet's visit during Passover.

In the ancient world, reclining while eating was a symbol of freedom, so reclining to the left for portions of the Passover meal is traditional. When eating the symbols of slavery, participants don't recline. The leader may wear a *kittel*, a white robe similar to priestly garments worn during the Temple service, but this is up to the individual's preference.

As with the foods, the exact order of the service may differ, but anyone interested in celebrating Passover can find books translating the Seder into Christian understanding, in addition to those from a strictly Jewish perspective.

Different traditions have grown up around Passover through time. Today's Seder plate is of fairly recent origin. The most popular arrangement of elements is from a sixteenth-century rabbi, Isaac Luria. Other customs are of similarly recent origin: eating hard-boiled eggs (sixteenth century) and the cup of Elijah (late seventeenth century).

The Passover is clearly about redemption and modern Jewish commentators often stress the Messianic nature of Passover. As one said, "Messianic hope would not be credible in the world as we know it were it not for the fact—rehearsed at Pesah—that redemption has occurred." For Christians, of course, Jesus fulfilled Messianic hope at a Passover two thousand years ago.

The most obvious connection of Passover to redemption is the lamb killed as a sacrifice. Scripture is clear about Jesus' identity as the Lamb of God. Recall John's recognition: "Look, the Lamb of God, who takes away the sin of the world!" (Jn 1:29). The Passover lamb was a visible symbol, preparing people for the coming of Jesus, who would perform the final sacrifice.

In Exodus, people are instructed to roast the lamb whole. Specifically, no bones were to be broken. When Jesus died on the cross, the Roman soldiers did not break His legs, as was common practice at the time to hasten death. As commanded, the final Passover Lamb—Jesus—remained whole.

The final tie between Jesus and the Passover lamb came from the cross. When Jesus was about to die, they "put the sponge on a stalk of the hyssop plant, and lifted it to Jesus' lips" (Jn 19:29). Much earlier, at the first Passover, God commanded the Israelites to use the hyssop plant to put the lambs' blood on the doorposts. Here the Romans used hyssop to give Jesus, the Lamb of God, a final drink while His blood was being shed.

Putting the Last Supper into its context as a Passover meal is more difficult, since the Gospels don't give us many details. Since the first and third cups of wine during the traditional Passover meal are the most important, some sources believe that these are the two cups mentioned in Luke. The cup Jesus gave His followers may well have been the first cup of Passover, which traditionally consecrated the meal.

The third cup was the cup of redemption, which was usually taken with a small piece of the *afikomen*. That celebrants took the bread and wine together at this point forms an obvious— though unproved—parallel to Jesus' institution of the Lord's Supper. The cup of redemption is also significant, as Jesus was offering Himself as the redemption for all.

The wine used in the celebration pulls the two more closely together as well. Passover wine should be blood red in color. The assertion of Jesus: "This cup is the new covenant in my blood, which is poured out for you," is more dramatic in the context of a blood red wine from the cup of redemption.

Another modern Jewish commentary underscored the Messianic nature of the Passover by explaining that the middle matzo, which is broken during the ceremony, represents the messianic redemption to come. Though how long this association has been in place is uncertain, it provides a parallel to Jesus breaking bread and saying, "This is my body given for you" (Lk 22:19). Was He breaking a piece of matzah that already symbolized messianic redemption? The action would be consistent with the kind of word-pictures Jesus used in teaching, but there is no way to know for sure.

Jesus entered Jerusalem on the day the sacrificial lamb was

traditionally chosen, which we now call Palm Sunday. His death on the cross took place during Passover at the hour of the final sacrifice. Jesus was buried at the beginning of the Feast of Unleavened Bread. This feast offered God thanks for life as symbolized by the bread that He provides. The Resurrection took place on the Feast of Firstfruits, a celebration of the beginning of harvest.

In addition, the Holy Spirit was sent at Pentecost (or Shavuot), the second of the three great Jewish feasts. Shavuot was also a harvest celebration, just as Jesus had predicted there would be a great harvest of believers. About three thousand believed on that first Pentecost, and the harvest continues. God provided the feasts to point the way to the fulfillment that came in Jesus' death, burial, and resurrection.

May

Sweet child of May you'll taste the caress
of Emerald's promised happiness.

Birthstone: Emerald
Birthstone Virtue: Discovers false friends and insures true love
Flower: Lily of the Valley

As with April, the origin of the name is uncertain, but it may refer to Maria, goddess of springtime growth. The name may also refer to the Majores branch of the Roman senate.

National Day of Prayer
Date varies—first Thursday in May

Prayer came to America with the first Puritan settlers, who quickly established it as a part of American life. The Continental Congress issued the first call to national prayer, requesting the colonies to pray for wisdom in forming a nation. President Lincoln followed a familiar tradition when he proclaimed a day of humiliation, fasting, and prayer in 1863.

This background made Congress' joint resolution in 1952, setting a national day of prayer a natural move. President Harry Truman signed the resolution into law. President Ronald Reagan amended the resolution in 1988, changing the day from "a suitable day each year, other than Sunday" to "the first Thursday in May in each year."

Observances vary across the United States, though the National Day of Prayer Task Force provides materials to guide interested groups in planning services. The day isn't just for Christians, but encourages people from all faiths to join in praying for America.

Mother's Day
Date varies—second Sunday in May

What kind of memories do you have of Mother's Day from your childhood? Was your church one that recognized all mothers in the congregation in some way? Perhaps you remember needing to have the right color corsage for both you and your mother. Somehow May flowers and honoring mothers go together naturally.

While the American holiday is fairly new, the idea of a day set aside to honor mothers isn't new. Both the Greeks and Romans held festivals to honor mothers. For a more modern example, people in England celebrate the fourth Sunday of Lent as Mothering Sunday.

The roots of the American Mother's Day go back to the Civil War. Many different people started celebrations designed to honor mothers in some way before we adopted our current celebration.

Anna M. Jarvis was the most directly responsible for today's celebration. On May 9, 1907, the second anniversary of her mother's death, she invited friends to her home in Philadelphia. There she outlined plans for making her mother's dream of a nationwide day to honor mothers a reality.

The next year, on May 10, 1908, church services honoring mothers were held in Grafton, West Virginia, and Philadelphia, Pennsylvania. For the service at the Andrews Methodist Church in Grafton, Miss Jarvis provided hundreds of carnations, her mother's favorite flower. Each mother and child in attendance received a carnation during the service.

Anna Jarvis continued working to promote her idea. In 1910, the governor of West Virginia issued the first Mother's Day proclamation. By 1911, churches held Mother's Day services in all fifty states.

In May 1913, the House of Representatives passed a resolution asking the president, the Cabinet, the members of both Houses and the officials of the federal government to wear a white carnation on Mother's Day. The House followed with a resolution recommending that the second Sunday in May be designated as Mother's Day.

Wearing carnations gradually changed, with red carnations a symbol of living mothers and white ones for mothers who had died. Though the symbolism is the same, people in the rural South used roses instead of carnations. This was a matter of practicality, not refusal to conform. In the days before florists, carnations weren't available, but roses bloomed in gardens everywhere during May.

The church where the first Mother's Day service was held, Andrews Methodist Church, became the International Mother's Day Shrine, which is open to the public.

Memorial Day
May 30

Nearly all cultures have customs to honor the dead. The Greeks held a March Commemoration of the Dead, while the Romans decorated graves with flowers to celebrate Parentalia. Other cultures included honoring the dead as part of new year's celebrations.

Our modern Memorial Day celebrations date back to the Civil War. In the early days, people often referred to that time as Decoration Day since decorating the graves with flowers was a major part of the ceremony. Though usually called Memorial Day now, decorating graves is still part of the observance.

No one is certain who held the first Memorial Day observance. Most likely people in the South held the first informal Memorials before the end of the war. Many of the war dead lay buried in the South, where most of the battles were fought.

The official holder of the title "first Memorial Day" is Waterloo, New York. Druggist Henry C. Welles suggested their celebration and Union general John B. Murray approved it. He also gathered support from veterans and formed a committee to plan the ceremonies. The town honored its war dead on May 5, 1866.

Boalsburg, Pennsylvania is another leading contender for the honor of hosting the first Memorial Day. An informal memorial in 1864 became an established tradition by 1869.

One of the best-publicized early memorials took place at Columbus, Mississippi on April 25, 1866. After placing flowers on the Confederate graves, the women turned spontaneously and put magnolia blossoms on the graves of the Union soldiers. News of their action spread and appeared in the *New York Tribune.* It inspired the poem, "The Blue and the Gray," written by Francis Miles Finch, which was reprinted in many newspapers.

In turn, this publicity helped to heal the breach between the North and South following the end of the Civil War and led to the custom spreading throughout the United States.

An organization of Union veterans, the Grand Army of the Republic, suggested May 30 as a national Memorial Day in 1866. General John A. Logan, commander in chief, recommended that the arrangements be made to decorate the graves of Union soldiers throughout the country.

Memorial Day is now a legal holiday in all fifty states, though some of the southern states still celebrate older Confederate anniversaries in addition to Memorial Day. Since June 28, 1968, when President Lyndon Johnson signed legislation moving the dates to provide more three-day weekends, Memorial Day has been observed on the last Monday of May.

As America fought other wars after the Civil War, Memorial Day became a time to honor victims of each additional war as well. Official ceremonies still remember the war dead, but Memorial Day has now become a time to remember all those who have gone before, not just those who died in wars.

June

Pearls for the girls of June, the precious wealth,
and to crown it all they bring her health.

Birthstone: Pearl, Moonstone
Birthstone Virtue: Wealth
Flower: Rose

Juno, Roman goddess of marriage and women, provided the name for June.

Pentecost
Date varies—May/June

You may be familiar with Pentecost as the time at which the Holy Spirit came to the first believers after Christ's ascension. The focus is mainly on the descent of the Holy Spirit, but it also marks off the first Christian assembly. You can consider Pentecost as the birthday of the church. *Pentecost* comes from the Greek *pentekoste* or "the fiftieth," because it comes fifty days after Passover.

Early Christians linked Pentecost and Easter so closely that the period was one season of rejoicing. Joy has always been such a major part of this celebration that the Council of Nicaea forbade both kneeling and fasting during Pentecost as being too penitential.

You still might see the names Whitsun or Whitsunday for Pentecost. In Britain, baptisms were common on this day. This may have been because Pentecost was part of the Easter season, or for the more practical reason that the streams and rivers had warmed enough to allow outdoor baptisms. From "White Sunday," after the new converts' baptismal robes, the name became contracted into Whitsunday.

People in the Middle Ages made Pentecost a major celebration. They used a wooden, painted dove about the size of a cart wheel to represent the Holy Spirit. The painting was usually a white dove against a blue background broken by golden rays. During the service, a "Holy Ghost Hole" opened in the church ceiling and the dove swung in circles as it descended to hang over the congregation. In some services, people dropped red roses for the tongues of fire and water for baptism.

In a few churches, people dropped burning straw balls or wicks from the ceiling to represent the tongues of fire. They suspended this custom for obvious reasons. In other churches, particularly in France, trumpets called to mind the rushing of the wind when the Spirit came.

During the thirteenth century in France, many cathedrals released white pigeons through the hole. The birds became living symbols of the Holy Spirit, while roses fell symbolizing the tongues of fire. Unfortunately, using live pigeons left worshippers vulnerable to unwanted side effects.

Though the older customs have been discontinued, many churches still use red as the liturgical color for Pentecost. Tongues of fire are a symbol of Pentecost, as is the descending dove.

Shavuot
Date varies—May/June

Had you been a first-century Jewish believer, you would have known Pentecost as Shavuot or the Feast of Weeks. At that time, people often used the term "Pentecost" to refer to the entire fifty days proceeding the actual day of celebration, a practice the early Christians continued. The alternate term, "Feast of Weeks," came from the fact that people figured the day by counting seven weeks after Pesach (Passover).

Shavuot marked the end of the grain harvest and the beginning of the next agricultural season when the fruit began to ripen. During the celebration, priests offered two loaves of leavened bread as a thanksgiving to God and a prayer for a successful harvest.

Over the years, new customs arose to celebrate Shavuot, including decorating with green plants, branches, and trees and eating dairy foods. No one knows for sure where these customs started, though using plants may be a remembrance of the first fruits once brought to the temple.

Modern Judaism still celebrates Shavuot. On many kibbutzim in Israel, people hold various religious and secular celebrations of the first fruits similar to the original observance. They have processions, and dance and sing to celebrate the fruits of the land.

Reform Jews celebrate confirmation on Shavuot, a tradition borrowed from Christianity. They feel that an individual isn't fully prepared to accept the responsibilities of adulthood at the traditional age of thirteen for the Bar Mitzvah. In some cases, confirmation supplements the Bar Mitzvah and in others, takes the place of it. During confirmation, boys and girls in their late teens accept the responsibilities of following Jewish tradition and become full adult members of their congregations.

Father's Day
Date varies—third Sunday in June

Looking at Father's Day from a modern perspective, you might think having a day for fathers is logical if you're going to have one for mothers. A look at history shows a different story. Mother's Day inspired Father's Day, but Father's Day took more time to catch on.

Central Church of Fairmont, West Virginia, celebrated the first recorded Father's Day. Mrs. Charles Clayton suggested the observance to her pastor, Dr. Robert T. Webb. He agreed, and the church held a service to honor fathers on July 5, 1908.

Despite this, people usually credit Sonora Louis Smart Dodd of Spokane, Washington, with originating the idea in 1909, because the observance spread beyond her church. Her inspiration came from the already existing Mother's Day and her own father. William Smart had lost his wife in childbirth and was left to raise his daughter and five sons alone.

Mrs. Dodd saw the celebration as centered on the church, so she discussed the idea with her minister, Dr. Rasmus. He approved the idea and helped her to take it to Reverend Conrad Bluhm, president of the Spokane Ministerial Association, and the Spokane Minister's Alliance. The city's YMCA also agreed to help sponsor the celebration.

The mayor of Spokane released a Father's Day proclamation, as did the Governor of Washington, M. E. Hay. Mrs. Dodd would have preferred June 5, her father's birthday, for the first observance, but the date didn't leave enough time to plan festivities. Therefore, they held the celebration on the third Sunday, June 19, 1910, still within his birth month.

The organizers took part of their observance from Mother's Day, with single red roses worn for living fathers and single white ones for fathers who had passed away. Mrs. Dodd's efforts to honor fathers received newspaper coverage throughout the nation.

Across the country, other people had the same idea independently. As early as 1915, Harry C. Meek began working to establish Father's Day. He arranged a celebration in 1920, also on the third Sunday in June, as this was the Sunday nearest his birthday, June twenty-fifth.

The idea continued to spread, but was still slow to be declared an official holiday.

Senator Margaret Chase Smith was a major proponent of designating an official Father's Day. She insisted that singling out only one parent for honor, rather than recognizing both, was an insult. She also suggested that Congress was at fault in not choosing to honor fathers before this time. Finally, in 1972, President Richard Nixon signed a congressional resolution fixing the day permanently.

July

The ruby stole a spark from heaven above,
to bring the July maiden fervent Love.

Birthstone: Ruby
Birthstone Virtue: Insures forgetfulness or cure of any ills
 arising from love or friendship
Flower: Larkspur

As mentioned earlier, July was named for Julius Caesar.

Independence Day
July 4

You're probably familiar with the story of the American Revolution. Many history books tell our nation's struggle for independence from Great Britain. Here are some interesting additions to that story.

July 4 almost wasn't designated Independence Day. In 1777, the year immediately following the adoption of the Declaration of Independence on July 4, many leaders thought July 2 was the logical date to remember.

Richard Henry Lee had brought the issue of independence before the Continental Congress on June 7, 1776. Attending as a delegate from Virginia, Lee had the support of John Adams in advancing his motion: "Resolved, that these United Colonies are, and of right ought to be, free and independent States, that they are absolved from all allegiance to the British Crown, and that all political connection between them and the State of Great Britain is, and ought to be, totally dissolved."

During the debate over the resolution, Congress appointed a committee to draft a declaration of independence. On July 2, the Lee Resolution passed, thereby dissolving ties with Great Britain and establishing American independence. The Declaration itself was a formal statement of the intent of the Lee Resolution.

Philadelphia celebrated independence with bells, bonfires, and fireworks in 1777, on July 2. Sailors fired salutes from ships in the harbor and people placed candles in the windows of their homes. Congress adjourned for the day, as it has for Independence Day celebrations since. The next year, in 1778, the day was changed to July 4. Dr. David Ramsay of Charleston, South Carolina claimed to have delivered the first Fourth of July speech. In years following, speeches and addresses became the focal point of most celebrations.

The first overseas celebration of America's independence occurred at a dinner party in Paris, France on July 4, 1778. John Adams noted in his diary that he and Benjamin Franklin met with other Americans in Paris and a few Frenchmen to remember the Declaration of Independence.

In 1781, Massachusetts became the first state officially to recognize Independence Day as a holiday. Other states gradually adopted the celebration, which then spread westward with the nation's expansion.

In an odd twist, on the fiftieth anniversary of American independence (July 4, 1826), both Thomas Jefferson and John Adams died. Five years later (July 4, 1831), James Monroe died. People at the time saw the deaths of the early leaders on the anniversary of independence as significant.

August

The August maiden with sweet simplicity
wears sardonyx, gem of felicity.

Birthstone: Sardonyx, Peridot
Birthstone Virtue: Married happiness
Flower: Gladiolus

Augustus Caesar gave his name to August.

September

Out of the depths shall sapphires come
brings September's child wisdom.

Birthstone: Sapphire
Birthstone Virtue: Frees from enchantment, repentance
Flower: Aster

Named from the days when September was the seventh
month in the calendar, the name comes from the Latin *septem*
or seven.

Labor Day
Date varies—First Monday in September

After the Civil War, labor became a growing problem in the United States. Most laborers had little contact with management and no one to help them when disputes came up. Owners had no concept of fair treatment for their workers. The combination of being out-of-touch and, in many cases, callous treatment led workers to organize and form labor unions.

The idea of a specific day for labor followed. In 1882, at a meeting of an early labor organization—the Brotherhood of Carpenters and Joiners—Peter J. McGuire first proposed setting aside a day to honor labor. He shared his idea on a wider scale on May 8, 1882 during a meeting of the New York Central Labor Union.

Part of his idea included the date. He suggested the first Monday in September because it would be midway between Fourth of July and Thanksgiving, and the weather would be pleasant. He also proposed a street parade to "show the strength and *esprit de corps* of the trade and labor organizations," suggesting that the day end with a picnic or similar activity.

The Central Labor Union approved his idea, and people celebrated the first Labor Day in New York City on September 5, 1882. This was a Tuesday but they changed the observance to the recommended Monday within two years.

The activities of the day closely resembled McGuire's original plan. Ten thousand workers marched up Broadway from City Hall to Union Square, carrying banners and escorted by bands. At the end of the march, participants went to Reservoir Park for a picnic, concert, and speeches.

The idea quickly gained acceptance. Only two years later, in 1884, the Federation of Organization Trades and Labor Unions, the future AFL, endorsed the idea and groups celebrated in cities throughout the Northeast. By 1895, events took place across the nation.

Oregon was the first state to recognize Labor Day as a legal holiday on February 21, 1887. They set aside the first Saturday in June until 1893, when lawmakers moved the celebration to the first Monday in September. The same year, New Jersey approved the first Monday in September.

By 1893, twenty more states had established Labor Day. The same year, Congress considered a bill to establish Labor Day as a national holiday. Both houses approved it and President Grover Cleveland signed it on June 28, 1874, making it a legal holiday for all federal employees. Eventually all the remaining states and Puerto Rico legalized the holiday.

From its beginnings in organized labor, Labor Day now honors all who work. It has become more of a family festival, providing a last celebration before the end of the summer, or one last getaway before settling down to school in the fall.

Rosh Hashanah
Date varies—September/October

Many think of Rosh Hashanah as the Jewish New Year, but this is a more recent idea. Scripture designates this as a day of rest (see Lev 23:24) but the Bible gives few details about this holiday. Over the years, the celebration of Rosh Hashanah became tied to the creation of the world, in addition to a new year. Rosh Hashanah comes at the beginning of a month with two major Jewish holidays: the Day of Atonement (Yom Kippur) and the Feast of Booths (Sukkot). It is also the first of ten penitential days ending with Yom Kippur. The combination lent itself well to a New Year focus.

Unlike most other Jewish holidays, people celebrate Rosh Hashanah mostly at the synagogue. They celebrate God's kingship as well as His judgment. They believe that on Rosh Hashanah, God opens three different record books showing everyone's deeds: for those who are completely wicked; for those who are completely righteous; and for those in between.

God immediately seals the righteous for life and the wicked for death. Judgment for the middle group is suspended until Yom Kippur. During the month before Rosh Hashanah, a traditional greeting is "May you be inscribed for a good and sweet year." Some may add "May you be inscribed and sealed for a good life" between Rosh Hashanah and Yom Kippur. Others avoid this after the first night of Rosh Hashanah to keep from suggesting that the person hasn't already been inscribed.

Blowing the shofar—or ram's horn trumpet—is the only part of the celebration specifically mentioned in the Scripture. Meditations or verses called *piyyutim* are popular during the observance of Rosh Hashanah. In keeping with the theme of the holiday, most focus on the power of God.

Yom Kippur
Date varies—September/October

Yom Kippur—the Day of Atonement—is the holiest day of the Jewish calendar. It is a day of fasting and repentance considered the "Sabbath of Sabbaths." God set aside the day for the people of Israel and gave Moses the celebration's details in Leviticus 16. He covered every aspect, from Aaron's dress to how the sacrifices should be presented, to sending the scapegoat into the wilderness.

The service consisted of three major confessions of sin. First, the high priest confessed sin and made atonement for himself and his household. Then he did the same for the community of priests. Finally, he offered confession and sought atonement for the entire Jewish people. The ritual of the scapegoat accompanied the final act.

After the destruction of the temple, the focus began to shift more to individual repentance. The modern "sacrificial service," *Avodah,* describes the service formerly done by the high priest.

People today include the souls of the dead in the celebration. Many visit cemeteries, lighting candles for the living and the dead. Services include a special *Yizkor* "He will remember" service in memory of the dead, ending with the confession of faith and blowing the shofar.

After Yom Kippur ends, the special break-the-fast dinner may include traditional foods such as challah, chicken soup, wine, honey or sponge cake, and *taglach*—a sweet pastry made with nuts, honey, and cinnamon.

Sukkot
Date varies—September/October

If you could visit Israel when people still worshipped in the temple, as autumn approached you would hear people speaking of "the Festival." People commonly referred to Sukkot, the third of the pilgrim feasts, as if it were the only festival. Everyone would know which festival you meant.

You probably know Sukkot by the name the Feast of Booths or the Feast of Tabernacles. After focusing on repentance at Yom Kippur, the mood switches to rejoicing at Sukkot. The Hebrew word *sukkot* is the plural of *sukkah* or booth.

Celebrating Sukkot comes in three parts: 1) the commandment to live in sukkot (or booths) for seven days; 2) gathering together the fruit and branches; and 3) rejoicing during the holiday. (See Lev 23:40, 42.)

A sukkah must be a true booth, not lower than five feet or higher than thirty feet. It must be roofed only with leaves or straw, and must be built new every year.

According to one source, the booth's fragility symbolized the brevity and insecurity of human life. It reminded Jews of the time they spent wandering in the wilderness and how dependent they are on God.

Another part requires using the branches of different trees to rejoice before the Lord. The traditional plants now used are citron, a palm branch, a sprig of myrtle, and a willow branch. People shake the four together in all four directions, upwards and downwards. A variety of interpretations exist. Some tie the plants to the prayer for rain. Others claim the four species represent the four Patriarchs: Abraham, Isaac, Jacob, and Joseph.

On the last day of the ancient celebration, a water offering took place. A priest filled a golden vessel at the Pool of Siloam and carried it in procession to the temple altar. There he transferred the water to a silver container and poured it on the altar through a spout. He then offered a prayer for rain.

It was probably during this offering that Jesus stood and said, "If a man is thirsty, let him come to me and drink... streams of living water will flow from within him," (Jn 7:37-38). At a time when the people of Israel prayed for rain, Jesus offered Himself as Living Water.

October

October's child in darkness oft may grope,
the iridescent opal bids it hope.

Birthstone: Opal, Tourmaline
Birthstone Virtue: Misfortune and Hope
Flower: Calendula

October's name also comes from its former position in the calendar. The Latin *octo* means eight.

Clergy Appreciation Day
Date varies—second Sunday in October

Clergy Appreciation Day is one of the newest holidays, but has grown explosively during its short lifetime. The idea grew out of a "Pastor of the Year" contest in 1991, held by Under His Wing ministries, led by Jerry Frear. He wrote ten states in 1992 to request state declarations. Eight out of the ten responded, and 110 churches held celebrations. In 1993, twenty-one states declared Clergy Appreciation Day and thirty thousand churches participated. Articles appeared in magazines and interviews aired on Christian radio.

In 1994, Focus on the Family began to promote Clergy Appreciation for the entire month of October, although they do recommend the second weekend of the month for churches preferring to observe a single weekend. Focus on the Family prepares a revised planning guide each year to help congregations.

DaySpring Cards joined the effort in 1995 by creating a line of cards for clergy and their spouses. They also provided Christian retailers with materials to support the celebration.

The observance has continued to grow. Forty-nine out of the fifty states now proclaim the second Sunday of October as Clergy Appreciation Day. Approximately one-third of the nation's churches participate every year. In 1998, Australia joined in recognizing clergy.

Because Scripture states that Christians should honor leaders, clergy appreciation has been around informally for years, as congregations have chosen anniversaries or other times for recognition.

Halloween
October 31

Over the years, Halloween has become one of the most troublesome holidays for Christians to celebrate. We get the name *Halloween* from "All Hallow's Eve" or the evening before All Saint's Day. While it is usually considered Druidic in origin, additional customs blended into the observance from Roman tradition.

The Celtic tribes considered November 1 as New Year's Day. When the Romans conquered Britain and began imposing their customs, three celebrations fell on the same day: festivities for the Roman sun god, the goddess Pomona, and Samhain (pronounced Sow´en). Most of the traditions remained Celtic, but sacrifices to the sun god also became a part of the celebrations.

At Samhain, people celebrated Cernunnos, the Celtic god of the underworld. Artist often depicted Cernunnos with antlers, leading Christians to identify him with Satan. In Celtic tradition he wasn't associated with evil in the sense that Satan is. In addition to being the god of the underworld, he was the god of plenty. The Celts believed that Cernunnos judged the souls and decided their fate during Samhain.

Roman worship of Pomona also shaped the festivities. She was the goddess of orchards and the harvest. The festival in her honor featured apples, nuts, grapes, and other fruits. These features have come down to today in the form of apple bobbing and, until recently, using nuts to tell fortunes.

The "All Hallow's Eve" portion of Halloween was not added until later. All Saints Day—or All Hallows Day—was not celebrated close to Samhain until the eighth century. At that time, Pope Gregory III moved the church festival to November 1.

On that date he dedicated a chapel in Rome in honor of All Saints. In the next century, Pope Gregory IV decreed All Saints' Day to be a universal church observance.

By the Middle Ages, people had accepted the idea of All Hallows Eve as the favorite time of witches and sorcerers. The idea of witches flying on broomsticks developed during this time period, with All Hallow's Eve being the most important of the witches' sabbaths.

The roots of modern Halloween parties go back to this time. To avoid facing evil alone, people gathered together and told of strange or spooky experiences to pass the time and they played traditional games such as bobbing for apples.

American observance of Halloween came fairly late, as most early settlers were Protestant. They left saints' days behind them along with any folk customs attached to them. Only a few scattered and regional observances of Halloween took place. That changed with the Irish potato famine and the resulting wave of immigration in the 1840s. Most of the immigrants were Catholic, bringing both the religious observances and the folklore remnants of Samhain with them.

Halloween became a national observance in the United States by the late 1800s, a time for adult parties. Like many earlier harvest-related parties, Halloween gatherings often served to allow courting between young people. Divination games became popular, especially to predict future mates. Party hosts and hostesses converted basements into the first haunted houses at Victorian Halloween parties. Costumes appeared for the first time as magazines detailed suggestions for successful parties and gave ideas for invitations, decorations, and activities.

By the beginning of the twentieth century, a new realism began to take over the previous preoccupation with entertainment and the supernatural. As the times changed, so did the celebration of Halloween. New books focused on the fun elements of Halloween for children. Party books gave instructions on entertainment appropriate for children, avoiding elements that might be too frightening. Scavenger hunts and musical chairs replaced matchmaking.

The custom of Mischief Night survived the changes, and most people were tolerant of innocent pranks. As time passed, though, Mischief Night had become more than harmless fun. Vandalism began occurring under the guise of mischief. One answer was to hold a Halloween party to keep potential mischief-makers occupied. The first individual parties designed to prevent problems on Halloween date back to 1908.

By the time World War II ended, Halloween had become a children's holiday. Though vandalism was still an occasional problem, much of the "Mischief Night" idea vanished. As communities grew, citywide parties became impractical. The focus switched to the classroom and the home. School classes celebrated Halloween and mothers planned in-home parties for their children.

Halloween is a time of celebration for modern day pagans. Various neo-pagan groups celebrate both Beltane and Samhain as one of two great festivals of the year.

Costumes. Wearing costumes on Halloween has a variety of possible explanations. You may be able to look back to the pagan new year's feast where villagers greeted ghosts with a banquet. At the end of the feast, the inhabitants wore masks and costumes representing the souls of the dead as they paraded to the outskirts of town leading the ghosts away.

Another explanation is that costumes may stem from the

practice of displaying saints' relics on All Hallows. In poor churches that couldn't afford relics, some parishioners dressed as patron saints, with the remainder of the congregation as angels or devils. Even this change may well have come from old memories of dressing as the dead to lure ghosts away.

More recent costumes reflect modern culture. In the 1920s children's costumes reflected the various images and interests of the decade: Charlie Chaplin, cowboys, Indians, and clowns. By the 1950s, the media began to play a role in costume selection. Little girls began dressing as princesses, brides, and angels, while boys might be army men or hoboes. Through the years since then, each popular movie, television show, or toy line begets a multitude of miniature replicas each Halloween.

The familiar black and orange colors of Halloween come from the different parts of its development. Black is a traditional color representing death, while orange comes from the color of ripening fruit like pumpkins.

Trick-or-treating. Trick-or-treating is likewise obscure. It is most similar to an ancient Irish practice on Halloween when groups of peasants went from house to house asking for money to buy delicacies for a feast.

The groups requested contributions in the name of Muck Olla, a druid deity, or St. Columba, patron saint of Ireland. They promised prosperity to the generous and threatened the stingy.

In America, trick-or-treating became popular between 1920 and 1950. It began in the wealthier parts of the East and spread from there throughout the West and South.

Jack O'lantern. Jack O'lantern, while familiar today as a symbol of Halloween, doesn't seem to have the same background as other symbols. Although Celtic in origin, it doesn't seem to be connected with the celebration of Samhain.

There are several variations of Jack's story. One story says that he tricked the Devil into climbing an apple tree to get an apple. Then he cut a cross into the tree to keep him from climbing back down. Once he had the Devil trapped, Jack made him promise he would never come for Jack's soul or claim it in any way.

When Jack died, heaven rejected him, but when he tried to enter hell, the Devil turned him away, as he had promised never to take Jack's soul. With both heaven and hell closed to him, Jack was left stranded and doomed to wander the earth eternally.

As a parting gift, the Devil threw Jack a coal from the fires of hell to light his way. Jack had been eating a turnip, so he put the coal inside. Ever since, he has been traveling the earth with his lantern. Over time, people used other vegetables besides turnips, including rutabagas, potatoes, and the now-familiar pumpkin.

November

Born in November happy is she,
whom the topaz teaches fidelity.

Birthstone: Topaz
Birthstone Virtue: Fidelity and Friendship
Flower: Chrysanthemum

November is another of the "number named" months, taking
its name from the Latin *novem* or nine.

All Saints' Day
November 1

As early as the fourth century, people suggested that a special day be set aside to commemorate all the martyrs. Some Christians suffered martyrdom in groups or their names weren't individually known. The year wasn't long enough to have a separate day for each martyr.

Eastern churches have observed various dates since the fourth century. St. John Chrysostom preached a sermon every year to venerate all the saints. The holy day began in the Roman church when Pope Boniface IV consecrated the Pantheon in Rome in A.D. 609. Formerly the temple to all the old Roman gods, he dedicated it to the Virgin Mary and all the martyrs. Yearly observances began in May 610.

Pope Gregory III changed the date from May to November during the consecration of the chapel at St. Peter's Basilica and expanded the remembrance to include all saints, not just martyrs. Though some have stated that this change was to Christianize or overshadow the lingering remnants of Samhain, other scholars argue that a more practical reason inspired the change. Celebrating on November 1 allowed the many pilgrims coming to Rome for the feast to be fed from the fall harvest.

In A.D. 830, Pope Gregory IV established the feast in the church calendar as All Saints' Day. He required all Catholics to observe it, including the vigil of preparation on All Hallow's Eve.

Thanksgiving
Date varies—fourth Thursday in November

Setting aside a day to offer thanks goes back to Greek festivals for Demeter or Roman ones for Ceres. Anglo-Saxons celebrated a "harvest home" with a feast. In Scotland a *kirn* included special church services and a large dinner. For Jews, the eight-day Feast of Tabernacles provides an opportunity to offer God thanks.

The first American settlers knew about thanksgiving from both Christian and non-Christian traditions, but the first thanksgivings in America came from Christian traditions. The Feast of St. Martin of Tours, or Martinmas may have inspired the first thanksgiving.

During medieval times, the feast was an almost universal harvest and thanksgiving celebration held on November eleventh. The festive meal featured roasted goose. Celebrants drank St. Martin's wine—the first made from newly harvested grapes.

Though most people now think of Plymouth, Massachusetts when they think of the first Thanksgiving, a variety of other sites around the country also claim the honor of holding the first Thanksgiving in America.

Modern Americans think of thanksgiving in terms of the holiday feast. For the Pilgrims at Plymouth, a thanksgiving was one of three allowable holy days: the Sabbath, the Day of Humiliation and Fasting, and the Day of Thanksgiving and Praise. They also celebrated successful harvests, but in their minds the harvest celebration and a thanksgiving were two different events.

What is generally regarded as the first official thanksgiving took place at Plymouth Colony in 1621. Though they didn't record a date, they must have held celebration between September 21 and November 9, when the *Fortune* arrived with new settlers.

Undoubtedly, the colonists offered a prayer of thanksgiving for the meal, even though the celebration was not an official thanksgiving. Today, we often call this a table grace from the Latin *gratiae* or *thanks*.

The Pilgrims probably considered that event a harvest celebration. Though a day of thanksgiving might conclude with a feast, the participants wouldn't have indulged in the games and other recreations played at the first celebration. The first official declared Thanksgiving, a holy day set aside for giving thanks, took place in 1623, after rain saved the colony's crops.

Nationally, the Continental Congress declared the first Thanksgiving in 1777. At this time, the difference between a harvest celebration and thanksgiving was obvious. The proclamation specifically stated that it was a solemn occasion. Over the years, presidents declared various other thanksgivings until the custom fell out of use after 1815.

President Lincoln reestablished the tradition in 1863 when he declared two Thanksgivings, one on Thursday, August 6, and the other for the last Thursday in November. Eventually, Lincoln's choice of the last Thursday in November became the traditional date. Congress passed legislation in 1941 making the fourth Thursday of November a national holiday.

Over the years, giving thanks and a harvest festival have blended to form our modern celebration. Even football games played on Thanksgiving have their roots in the shooting contests and other games from the first Thanksgiving.

Turkey. The familiar Thanksgiving turkey may have been present at the first feast, but since other meat and fish is also mentioned, the turkey probably wasn't the centerpiece of the meal. The word *turkey* for our American bird came with the Pilgrims. In England, *turkey* meant a guinea fowl. Traders imported the bird into England from Turkey. Eventually it acquired the country's name. When the colonists saw the similarity to the American bird, they gave it the same name.

Pilgrims. Each year, school children dress as black and white Pilgrims. The first settlers would be surprised and bewildered to see their modern appearance. Buckles appeared as decorations later in the seventeenth century, after the time the Pilgrims settled Plymouth. Artists have exaggerated the collars and cuffs in our modern conception of Pilgrim dress. The women's aprons would have been larger than those usually shown on the "typical" Pilgrim. Not all of the settlers wore black, except on Sundays and special occasions, since they associated black with dignity and formality. For everyday wear, they dressed in the colors and fashions that others of similar station wore.

One of the biggest changes, though, would be in the name itself. The name *Pilgrim* didn't become common until the mid-nineteenth century. The Pilgrims would have called themselves Separatists or Puritans when speaking of their faith. They called each other *saints,* while other colonists who made up their group were called *strangers.*

Indians. The Native people living in Massachusetts when the Puritans first arrived are included in most Thanksgiving pictures. Many pictures show them with the feathered bonnets of the Plains Indian tribes. The Wampanoag had a tribal culture quite different from the Plains Indians. Though they did use animal skins for clothing, they didn't wear feathered bonnets.

A teepee is out of place in a Thanksgiving picture, too. The Wampanoag built conical wigwams or *weetos* from cattails. The weetos varied in size, with larger ones built for families that might house up to fifty people.

Cornucopia. Next to the turkey and the pilgrims, the "horn of plenty" or cornucopia is one of the best-known symbols of Thanksgiving. Unlike the other symbols, it has roots in Greek and Roman mythology. The cornucopia represented the unending gifts the gods give mortals. Artists showed it with fruit and other gifts flowing freely from it.

The term *cornucopia* is from the Latin *cornu copiae*, which simply means "horn of plenty," the other commonly used name.

December

December's child shall live to bless
the turquoise that insures success.

Birthstone: Turquoise, Zircon
Birthstone Virtue: Great success and happiness, prosperity in
love
Flower: Narcissus

The last of the months named for numbers, our twelfth
month was named from the Latin *decem* or ten.

Hanukkah
Date varies—November/December

Since Hanukkah is close to Christmas, many Christians know the name. Hanukkah is actually an extrabiblical holy day. The Hanukkah story, which took place between the Old and New Testaments, comes from the apocryphal books First and Second Maccabees and the writings of Josephus.

While Israel was under Greek control, Antiochus Epiphanes outlawed all Jewish rituals and the worship of Greek gods replaced temple worship. While some Jews did bow to pressure, others resisted and died as martyrs. The turning point came when a group of Greeks came to the village of Modin and set up an altar.

An old priest, Mattathias, and his five sons fought the Greeks, fled to the mountains, and began a guerrilla war. Before dying, Mattathias turned leadership over to his son, Judah the Maccabee. Eventually, he and his followers retook Jerusalem and reclaimed the temple.

The Greeks had defiled the temple, and Judah could find only one small container of oil to light the temple menorah. The container had just enough oil for one day, but the menorah burned for eight days. The celebration of Hanukkah focuses on the Maccabees' successful fight for independence and the miracle of the oil.

Some sources leave out the miracle of the oil entirely. Perhaps the differing accounts depend on the focus of those telling the story. Despite the historical difficulties, Hanukkah remained a popular—though minor—festival.

The proximity to Christmas has influenced the celebration of Hanukkah, especially here in America. The tradition of giving children Hanukkah money is an old one, but gift giving has become a part of the holiday. Some give a small gift each of the eight nights of Hanukkah, while others choose to give only one larger gift.

The modern celebration of Hanukkah focuses on lighting the menorah. One candle is lit each night after sunset, adding a candle each night until all candles are lit on the eighth night. Oil is traditional for Hanukkah lights, but most people today use candles.

Games are another Hanukkah tradition, particularly the dreidel (or top). Games involve trying to spin the dreidel upside down or seeing how many you can spin at once. Trying to knock down other spinning dreidels is another favorite.

Because of the miracle of the oil, eating foods fried in oil is also customary. Traditional foods include potato latkes or *sufgainiyot*, a type of doughnut.

Advent
Date varies—November/December

Many Christians think of Advent as the four Sundays preceding Christmas. Others may think of the season as the days from December 1 to December 24, thanks to Advent calendars. For those in liturgical churches, Advent begins the church year, with the first Sunday of Advent always the one nearest the feast of St. Andrew the Apostle on November thirtieth.

The earliest record of a time set aside to prepare for Christmas is a decree issued by Bishop Perpetuus of Tours in A.D. 490. He required a fast held three days of every week from the Feast of St. Martin (November 11) to Christmas (December 25). At that time, the observance was called *Quadragesima Santi Martini* or the Forty Days' Fast of St. Martin.

Over the years, the practice spread, though Rome adopted Advent slowly. In the sixth century, Roman Christians began to celebrate Advent, but as a time of joyful celebration rather than one of penitence. During the reign of Pope Gregory in the sixth century, the four-week time period had become common. By the ninth century, the celebration was fairly universal in both Eastern and Western churches, though the length of time could still vary.

The two traditions, penitential and joyful preparation, remained separate for some time until an accident of history helped them join into one season. Some churches in Gaul (the area including modern day France) had begun to use liturgical books from Rome. Then Pope Stephen crowned Pepin as king. To honor the occasion, the new king commanded people to use the Roman liturgy throughout his kingdom.

Without a printing press, scribes hand copied the books. The lengthy process allowed the two themes in the celebration of Advent to remain mixed. When Charlemagne assumed the throne, he continued the effort, authorizing his advisor to write substitute portions for pieces missing from the books he had. The result was a true blend of the two traditions.

The blend might not have become widespread except for a decline in the Roman church during the tenth century. When the Roman emperors ordered a reform at the end of the century, they borrowed liturgical books from the north. What they received was the adapted liturgy. No one realized it had been changed, so they considered the blended liturgy authentically Roman. The mixture of joy and penitence for Advent became the liturgy for the whole medieval Roman church.

We get the word Advent from the Latin *adventus*, meaning coming or arrival. An old tradition says that the four weeks of advent represent the four comings of Christ: as a man, in a human heart, at the individual believer's death, and in the future at the Last Day.

Advent wreath. As with so many customs, we have Germany to thank for the Advent wreath. Pre-Christian customs associated with Yule celebrations, especially fires and lights, may be similar to using candles in Advent wreaths, but today's wreath developed long after the old pagan celebrations had been discontinued.

In fact, the custom of using lights as a symbol of Advent only dates to the sixteenth century. As fitting for Christmas preparation, the symbolism reminds people of the Old Testament when humanity remained in darkness waiting for the coming of Christ.

Wreaths are an ancient symbol of victory and glory. Using one in preparation for Christmas points to the coming of

Christ and the glory of His birth. The wreath can also point to the unending love of God. The evergreens used in the wreath are a reminder of the eternal life Jesus came to give.

Advent candles. The four candles placed on the wreath may vary in color. People use all purple or all blue, or a mixture of three purple and one pink.

Purple is the liturgical color for Advent. The pink candle symbolizes rejoicing and should be used for the third Sunday of Advent. Some churches call this Gaudete Sunday from the first word of that Sunday's Latin mass: *Gaudete* or "Rejoice." Using the two candle colors illustrates the mixture of penitence and joy in Advent.

The candles don't have fixed meanings. Some churches focus on themes such as love, peace, and joy. Others may look at characters from the Nativity story.

Some people add a white candle to the center of the wreath for the Christ Candle. Those who use five candles light one candle each of the four Sundays before Christmas, lighting the Christ Candle on Christmas Eve or Christmas Day.

The colors aren't as important as the symbolism of the flame: Christ coming as a light in the darkness. Using the traditional colors can add meaning, but the key is to remain focused on preparing to celebrate Jesus' birth.

St. Nicholas Day
December 6

We have little historical information about Nicholas despite the fact that he is well known today. He was born around A.D. 280, the son of wealthy parents. He became bishop of Myra in Asia Minor at thirty years of age and earned a reputation as a protector of the innocent.

During the Roman persecution, Emperor Diocletian had him imprisoned for this faith, but Emperor Constantine later freed him. According to historical records, Nicholas attended the Council of Nicaea. There clerics discussed whether Christ was divine or human. Nicholas argued for Christ's divinity.

Like many saints, a variety of stories grew up around his life, most of which are probably legendary. Some sources say Nicholas died on December 6, 343, while others say he died around 350, possibly on December sixth. His grieving parishioners buried him in Myra. His body remained there until 1087, when it was removed and taken to Bari, Italy, where it remains buried to this day.

In the twelfth century, French nuns began distributing candy to children on St. Nicholas' day. Gradually, the children believed St. Nicholas himself left the gifts if they had been good. Bad children received switches to frighten them into good behavior.

St. Nicholas' popularity continued to grow. In the Middle Ages, people named more churches for him than all the apostles together. They also began adding other details to St. Nicholas' story.

When he visited homes, a person dressed as St. Nicholas asked children questions about Scripture and the catechism, and whether they had been good or bad during the year.

Black Peter accompanied him and wrote the names of children who couldn't answer or who had been naughty. St. Nicholas then encouraged the children to do better before Christmas.

When the Protestant Reformation began, St. Nicholas was among the first traditions the new church dropped. Martin Luther knew it would be hard for people to give up customs like St. Nicholas, so he made a change instead. Rather than a saint, the gift giver became the *Christkindl* or Christ child. As an added touch, Jesus came on his own birthday, instead of St. Nicholas' day.

St. Nicholas came to America with Dutch immigrants. They also brought their term for him: *Sinter Klaas.* Just as the German *Christkindl* became Kriss Kringle, *Sinter Klaas* became anglicized as Santa Claus.

Santa Claus now overshadows the earlier St. Nicholas, a circumstance that would sadden him, but not because he wanted glory for himself. As a man of God, St. Nicholas would want people to remember Jesus at Christmas.

Christmas
December 25

During the Roman Empire, people usually celebrated the birthdays of rulers and other outstanding people, though not necessarily on the exact date of their birth. The early Christians' desire to honor Christ's birth may come from the fact that they gave him the title and other honors that pagans gave to the "divine" emperors. These Christians lived in a culture where the birth of a ruler was a major celebration. What could be more natural than celebrating the birth of the King of Kings?

Despite the logic of this, Christmas has long been surrounded by controversy. In A.D. 245, Origen wrote that even to consider observing it was a sin. Early Christians in Armenia and Syria accused Roman Christians of sun worship for celebrating Christmas on December twenty-fifth.

When Oliver Cromwell took power during the Commonwealth years in England, he banned the celebration of Christmas. The new laws required citizens to go about their business as usual on December twenty-fifth. When the Puritans settled America, they brought their distrust of Christmas with them, so Christmas wasn't celebrated at Plymouth. In 1659, Massachusetts made observance of Christmas a penal offense. However, the government repealed this law in 1681.

The first clearly recorded American celebration, though, was held in 1607 at Jamestown, Virginia. Forty of the one hundred original settlers commemorated the day in their wooden chapel. They experienced so many difficulties that they thought more about being thankful for their survival than celebrating Christmas.

Shortly after American independence, Elizabeth Drinker, a

Quaker, divided Philadelphia into three categories on how Quakers dealt with Christmas. The first were Quakers who "make no more account of it than another day." The second group celebrated the day as a religious observance, while the third "spend it in riot and dissipation." In those three divisions, she neatly summed up the way different groups viewed Christmas over the years.

As people settled the Southern states, Christmas came with them. Many gentlemen farmers fostered Christmas as both a sacred time and a time for relaxation. They kept many Old World traditions alive, including caroling, the Yule log, and decorative greenery. They added others such as fried oysters, eggnog, and a Christmas morning foxhunt.

In the South, Christmas became a time for a full house and a full larder. Thanks to the warmer Southern temperature, Christmas came not long after harvest season. This made a holiday break for rest and enjoyment even more natural. French settlers in Louisiana introduced firecrackers as a part of Christmas celebrations. The custom spread to other areas throughout the South, varied with shooting guns.

Christmas and the Sunday Schools. During the first half of the nineteenth century in America, Sunday schools helped promote the acceptance of folk customs such as the Christmas tree and Santa Claus. While they didn't deliberately do so, that was the end result of a curious division of thought about Christmas as a holy day and as a holiday. Because cultural customers such as the Christmas tree and Santa Claus fell outside the liturgical cycle and church year, people didn't see them as religious celebrations. But,

Sunday schools adopted what they saw as a pleasant and enjoyable celebration for children.

A wave of German immigration that peaked between 1850 and 1854 spurred acceptance. By 1859 Christmas trees were a frequent feature of Christmas in many Sunday schools. The customer then spread along with western expansion. Churches in settled areas sent donations of clothing and toys to frontier parishes along with their church papers. The publications gave details of Christmas celebrations like Christmas trees and Santa Claus visits. The frontier churches then followed the lead of their city counterparts. By the late 1860s Santa Claus began appearing at Iowa church suppers.

By the end of the nineteenth century, most churches had adopted Christmas as a holy day. Once churches accepted Christmas as Jesus' birthday, either actual of commemorated, concerns began growing about the folk customs. Some churches saw Santa and Christmas trees as encouraging greed and crowding Christ out of Christmas.

In response, churches began discarding the earlier customs and replacing them with programs that encouraged children to celebrate Jesus' birthday by giving him gifts that would then be given to charity. Other churches responded with programs focused on worship and drama.

As we enter the twenty-first century, the question still remains. Christmas today is the biggest holiday of the year, but Christians wonder how, or if, it should be celebrated. Both Sunday schools and individuals struggle with how to handle the variety of customs and traditions built around the celebration of Jesus' birth.

Christmas—The Year and the Date

A.D. 1? When Dionysius Exiguus reformed the calendar to reflect the birth of Christ, he dated the Nativity as occurring 753 years from the founding of Rome. He had the date right for the founding of Rome, but not for Jesus' birth. The mistake means that Jesus was born before *anno Domini*, "the year of our Lord." Since Herod the Great died in 4 B.C., and he is a major part of the Nativity story, Jesus must have been born some time before Herod's death. Some scholars estimate Jesus' birth at 5-4 B.C., while others suggest Jesus was born as far back as 8-7 B.C. Writing in A.D. 200, when Roman records were still accessible, Tertullian said that the birth of Jesus occurred seven or eight years before the supposed date.

Other attempts to pinpoint the year center around Luke's statement that the census that took Mary and Joseph to Bethlehem occurred "while Quirinius was governor of Syria." The problem with this is that records show Quirinius didn't become governor of Syria until A.D. 6-7. Though some use this to accuse Luke of inaccuracy, it is possible that Quirinius served an earlier term as governor.

Records available from the time show that the Roman Empire took censuses in fourteen-year intervals, with records existing from A.D. 20, 34, and 48. Counting back from these dates, there should have been censuses in A.D. 6 and 8 B.C. The latter date is possible for Jesus' birth.

December 25. Throughout the years, people have suggested different dates for Jesus' birth. Early Christian theologians in Egypt set the date as May twentieth. Other churchmen preferred late March or April, closer to Passover. Others chose January 1, coinciding with the New Year on the Roman calendar.

Scripture itself gives only a few clues. Shepherds were out-side with their sheep. This suggests the birth took place during the spring lambing season. Others point out that sheep can be seen in the fields year-round in the Middle East.

Over the years, the dates most frequently put forth were March 25, December 25, and January 6, which became Epiphany. December 25 may have been chosen for practical reasons, since that date coincides with winter solstice. Former pagan celebrations held on December 25 included Mesopotamian celebrations for Marduk, Greek ones for Zeus, and Roman *Saturnalia* in honor of Saturn.

Another possibility for choosing December 25 as Jesus' birthday stems from the fact that the church at this time believed that Jesus had died on March twenty-fifth. This idea came from the Jewish tradition of identifying the birth and death of patriarchs on the same day, in this case *birth* being conception. Nine months after March 25 is December twenty-fifth.

Others looked at the creation of the world to give a date for the Nativity, reasoning that the light of the physical and spiritual worlds would correspond.

They believed that the world had been created on March 25—the vernal equinox. Their conclusion came from the fact that day and night are equal at the equinox. Since God's division of day and night was perfect, he would have done so on that day. Again, December 25 is nine months from March twenty-fifth.

In an Italian (or African) writing from A.D. 243, *De Pascha Computus*, the author used the same logic, but decided on March 28 as Jesus' birth date, reasoning that God made the sun and moon on the fourth day of creation. Logically, then, the Sun of Righteousness would be born on the same day.

Once the date had become popularly accepted, many began looking for ways to prove that December 25 was the historical date of Jesus' birth. They made a number of assumptions based on the gospel accounts of the Nativity.

First, they assumed that Zechariah was serving in the Holy of Holies on the Day of Atonement, which would be around September twenty-fifth. Therefore, his son John would have been born on June twenty-fifth. Working from John's conception and the information the angel gave Mary at the Annunciation, Jesus would then have been conceived on March 25 and born on December twenty-fifth.

In the Roman world, people celebrated December 25 as *Natalis Solis Invicti*, the Birthday of the Unconquerable Sun. The festival honored Mithras, the sun god. Romans adopted Mithras from Persia, and the celebration gradually blended with *Saturnalia.*

Despite the similarity of the date, Christians were strongly aware of the differences between their celebration and those of the Romans. Church leaders rebuked new converts who kept using external symbols of sun worship.

We get the word *christmas* from England around 1050. People called the feast "Christes Maesse" or "Christ's Mass." The familiar *merry* in our "Merry Christmas" had a different meaning originally than it does now. When first used, *merry* meant "blessed, peaceful, or pleasant" rather than our current *joyful* or *happy*. In combination with *mass*, as in a church service, "Merry Christmas" pointed to spiritual blessings instead of a wish for a happy holiday.

The First Christmas—A Closer Look

When we think of Christmas, we have a certain image drawn from popular representations and songs. It is a pretty picture, but is it accurate? As with the date, Scripture gives few details.

The stable and the manger. Scripture tells us that Jesus lay in a manger. From this, many have assumed over the years that he must, therefore, have been born in a stable. This is a possibility.

From Scripture, we know there was no room at the inn at Bethlehem. Back then, a stable wasn't a separate wooden building but a cave. The area near Bethlehem is filled with caves, and people often used them to house livestock. The Church of the Nativity in Bethlehem, the traditional site of Jesus' birth, stands over one of these caves.

Over the years, the poor innkeeper has taken a lot of abuse for turning Mary away. The inn wasn't like our current motels with individual rooms. Most likely it was a one-story building where travelers slept together in a large room, perhaps with their animals.

During the census, with many people coming to Bethlehem, the inn would have been a noisy public place. The innkeeper may have shown Mary kindness in sending her to the stable where she could have more privacy. Possibly someone from the town invited them to bed down in a private stable.

The manger was probably not made of wood. People carved stone mangers into the cave's wall. In a home, the manger was the same mud brick as the house.

Swaddling clothes. Many modern nativity sets show Jesus with his arms stretched wide, as if reaching out to the world. This is a nice symbolic gesture, but it would have been impossible in reality. To wrap a child in swaddling clothes, the mother folded a square of cloth around the baby's body with the child's arms inside the cloth, too.

Once she had wrapped the child, she held the main cloth in place with bands that were four or five inches wide and five to six yards long. The band also went under the chin and across the forehead.

Shepherds. The Bible mentions shepherds and sheep regularly. Shepherds watched over their flocks night and day and protected them from wild animals. They cared for the sheep during lambing time, sheared them, and made sure they had enough to eat and drink.

At night, the shepherd would bring his flock within a sheepfold—a large, open, stone-walled pen. In a permanent sheepfold, shepherds might build a low shelter along one wall to provide extra protection for the flock.

Often shepherds put several flocks together in the sheepfold at night. The individual shepherds shared the task of watching over the flock. The next morning the shepherds easily divided their flocks. Each shepherd simply called his sheep to him.

There's no doubt that the shepherds were present at the Nativity, since Luke's Gospel records that they went at once to find the child. The interesting thing about the shepherds is that they *were* present. While caring for flocks had once been well regarded, shepherds had by this time become the outcasts of Jewish society. Being out in the fields for extended periods of time made it difficult for them to maintain ritual purity or attend synagogue services. In fact, shepherds weren't allowed to testify in court.

Some speculate that the shepherds mentioned in Luke were not general shepherds but those in charge of watching over the flocks raised for sacrifice at the temple. If this is true, it adds poignancy to their presence at Jesus' birth. The ones who raised the sacrificial lambs came to see the Lamb who would make the final sacrifice.

The wise men. While they are frequently referred to simply as "wise men," the word used for them is *magi*, from the Old Persian *magu*, referring to a hereditary class of priest-scholars. Neighboring Eastern countries also used the term, making it difficult to pinpoint their land of origin. They were probably astronomers, astrologers, or both. While they studied the stars as an astronomer would, they also believed that the movements of the stars foretold events on the earth.

At this time, there were two major groups of magi: the Persian and the Babylonian. The name itself comes from Persia, and early Christian tradition gave them Persian names and showed them in Persian garments. On the other hand, the Magi may have been Babylonians, since astronomy reached its highest development in Mesopotamia, and the star plays a major role in their visit.

Neither do we know how many came. The traditional number of three comes from the three gifts: gold, frankincense, and myrrh, listed in Matthew. People assumed each individual brought a different gift.

Another legend said that the wise men represented the three races of humanity descended from Noah's sons Ham, Shem, and Japheth. This provided additional reason for giving the number of Magi as three. The legend also explains why one of the Magi is traditionally shown as a black man.

Some believe that, because of the difficulty and danger of travel, an entire caravan may have traveled together to follow the star. With this theory, thirty or more magi are possible. Other theories have suggested anywhere from two to twelve.

Scripture refers to the wise men but doesn't mention how the magi traveled. Some saw their mounts as representing the three known continents. The horse came from Europe, the camel from Asia, and the elephant from Africa.

In the ninth century the names for the Magi became established. People knew them as Caspar (Gaspar or Jaspar), Melchior, and Balthasar. Other cultures had given them names, too. Artists began picturing them with crowns and in regal attire sometime after the eleventh century. Other legends grew up around them and their gifts.

The line between truth and fiction blurs three hundred years after their visitation, with their supposed bodies buried first in Constantinople and then in Cologne, Germany, as "The Three Kings of Cologne."

The star. What about the star the Magi followed? Turning to Scripture again, there is little detail. According to Matthew 2:1-12, the star went ahead of the wise men until it stopped over the house where Jesus lay.

Since people in biblical times didn't make distinctions among objects in the sky, this leaves us uncertain whether or not it was what we today would call a star. The Greek word used in Matthew's account—*aster*—can mean any luminous heavenly body.

People approach the star of Bethlehem in one of three ways: supernatural, rational, or historical viewpoint.

The supernaturalist looks at the account as literal history

and the star as a supernatural event created solely to herald Jesus' birth. It doesn't have a natural explanation and there is no need to attempt to explain the star, but simply to accept it. Since God created the star solely for the birth, it no longer exists today, as its purpose had been served.

The rationalist considers the entire story to be a myth with symbolic—rather than literal—meaning. They might suggest that the star was part of a story from another god that was transferred into the Nativity account.

The historical approach considers the story to be true, and looks at the star as a way to test its truth in the context of history. The goal is to locate astronomical evidence to support the appearance, much as Biblical archaeologists look for physical evidence to support events told in Scripture.

Those looking at the star from the third viewpoint have come up with a variety of different possibilities for what was the star of Bethlehem. While each of these does look for a natural explanation, finding one doesn't take away from the story. The timing of such a natural event would have to have been coordinated by God to mark Jesus' birth.

The first possibility is that the star was a large meteor. A more likely possibility, assuming a natural explanation, is that the star was a comet. Comets move slowly and are often visible for days. A comet can appear to "stand" over a location, and the tail can point at a particular location, both of which fit Matthew's record.

Yet another possibility is a new star or a nova. Though these aren't as conspicuous as comets or meteors, a nova is still a possibility. The last possibility is a conjunction of planets. Remember that the term *star* could have been used for anything seen in the sky and that the Magi were astronomers. In fact, the Magi thought the planets' movements could foretell events.

Another intriguing possibility is that the star was actually more than one of these possibilities. First, a conjunction of Jupiter and Saturn in 7-6 B.C. alerted the Magi to what was happening in Israel. Then, the comet of 5 B.C. reinforced the fact that something important was happening and sent them on their way. Finally, the comet of 4 B.C. appeared after they had reached Jerusalem and asked Herod for further information.

Christmas Symbols and Customs

Christmas trees. Using trees as part of religious celebrations goes back well beyond the first recorded Christmas tree. Egyptians erected green date palms indoors for winter solstice rites. Romans hung trinkets on pine trees during *Saturnalia* and used evergreens for *Natalis Solis Invicti*. In Britain, Druids placed candles, cakes, and gilded apples in tree branches as offerings.

Like many other customs, the idea of using a tree to celebrate Christmas seems to have been met with oppostion. In 575, Bishop Martin of Bracae forbade the use of all greenery. Christians didn't accept trees for home decoration until the sixteenth century. They did accept other greenery earlier. Both time and space separate trees used for the Christian celebration of Jesus' birth from older pagan customs.

The earliest story of how Christmas trees became part of Christian celebrations points to Boniface, an eighth-century English missionary known as the Apostle of Germany. He cut down an oak tree sacred to Norse god Odin, where the pagans had offered sacrifices and replaced it with an evergreen.

During the fifteenth century in Germany a variety of different religious plays—the so-called "mystery" plays—were popular. One of the props was a fir tree hung with apples to represent the Tree of the Knowledge of Good and Evil in the Garden of Eden. The connection with Christmas was natural since in the medieval church December 24 was Adam-and-Eve's Day.

When the church suppressed the mystery plays, the Paradise tree found its way into individual homes. Later, people added white wafers to the tree to represent the bread used in communion. This way, they paired apples representing the fall of man with symbols of the Body of Christ, the Redeemer of fallen man. In time, these led to cookies cut in a variety of shapes.

Probably the most familiar tale of all connected with the Christmas tree is the story of the Reformer, Martin Luther, walking home one winter evening. As he looked up, the stars in the sky shone through the branches of the evergreen trees and reminded him of the Star that shone over Jesus' birthplace. The evergreens drew him to think of the everlasting life Christ came to offer.

When he arrived at home, he cut down a small evergreen and brought it into his home. There he put candles on the branches as a reminder of the stars and of Jesus as light of the world. Others later adopted and expanded the custom and the Christmas tree was born.

Actually, candles weren't originally part of the tree. People displayed them on a separate decorated Christmas pyramid representing Christ as the Light of the World. As the tree gained popularity, the candles and other decorations moved from the pyramid to the tree sometime in the mid-seventeenth century.

The first Christmas trees were small enough to fit on a table with a crèche. Gradually, people began to use larger trees and the crèche went under the tree instead. The star displayed over the crèche moved to the top of the tree. Perhaps the alternate favorite tree-topper, an angel, can trace its roots to the same source.

The earliest recorded account of a Christmas tree is from 1605 in Strassburg, Germany. By the 1700s, the custom was firmly imbedded in Germany, and Christmas trees were mainly a German custom. When German settlers came to Pennsylvania in the early nineteenth century, they brought the Christmas tree with them.

President Franklin Pierce set up the first Christmas tree inside the White House in 1856. By 1877, the custom was well established. In 1923, President and Mrs. Calvin Coolidge began the custom of lighting the National Christmas tree on the White House grounds.

In England, Prince Albert popularized the Christmas tree in the 1840s. The English people had heard of Christmas trees before then, but his decision to set up a tree for his family spread the custom.

Early trees included small gifts for family members in addition to decorations. Most decorations at this time were homemade. Glass baubles began to replace homemade decorations around 1860. In the 1870s, the first mass produced ornaments began to appear. These were silver and gold embossed cardboard cutouts made in and around Dresden, Germany. Tinsel icicles made their way over from Nuremberg, Germany in 1878.

In 1895, electric lights replaced candles on President Cleveland's tree in the White House. Electric lights provided an important innovation, because candles had always been a fire hazard. Often, they were lit only once on Christmas Eve or Christmas Day while buckets of water and towels lay ready around the edges of the room in case of an accident.

In fact, candles were such a fire hazard that in 1908 several insurance companies announced they would no longer pay for fires started by trees and candles. They considered this to be a known risk taken by the policyholder, for which they weren't responsible. By 1920, candles had gone completely out of fashion.

Christmas cards. Several different items pre-dated our current Christmas cards. Early wall calendars carried seasonal wishes. Other forerunners included the visiting card or calling card, illustrated notepaper, and birthday greetings. All of these helped promote the later growth of Christmas cards by developing printing methods and mass production techniques.

One contender for the first Christmas card is a card designed by young London artist William Egley. The controversy comes from the fact that the date is blurred. It may have been dated 1842 or 1849.

Most sources recognized J. C. Horsley, a member of the Royal Academy, as having created the first card for Sir Henry Cole in 1843. Sir Henry found that he was too busy to write Christmas letters to his friends. He requested the card as an easier way to keep up his correspondence. At Horsley's suggestion, he printed extra copies of the card and offered them for sale. The card was lithographed and colored by hand, though presumably not by the busy Sir Henry.

Cards gradually became more popular in the 1860s, when members of the Royal Family began to commission artists for special holiday paintings. They had the paintings reproduced in color on Christmas cards. Later in the decade, London's Marcus Ward and Company began using artists to design Christmas cards. By 1870, the Christmas card was well established in England.

In America, the Christmas card developed a little later, though handwritten cards were common by the time of Andrew Jackson. Louis Prang is known as the father of the American Christmas card. Around 1875, he perfected a high quality lithographic color printing process and soon began making Christmas cards. Prang's cards were larger than those we often think of today, and the printing process he used made them frameable art pieces. Many people gave them instead of a small gift. He also began using classic artworks on his cards in an attempt to make art more familiar to people.

Around 1890, however, lower quality and less expensive cards began to be imported. Rather than lower his quality in order to lower price, Prang stopped producing cards.

Christmas candles. Some speculate that part of the imagery of Jesus as Light of the World, especially lighting candles or fires, goes back to the connection with sun worship. During *Natalis Solis Invicti* people of lower station considered candles an appropriate gift to those of higher station. According to R. T. Hampson, writing in England in 1841, this idea was still around then.

In Scandinavia, a large candle burned as a companion to the Yule log from Christmas Eve to Twelfth Night, representing the divine light that had come into the world. In Norway, people burned two lights every evening until New Year's Day.

One source stated that the modern custom of lighting Christmas candles came from Ireland. Legend states that the candles guided Mary and Joseph to a home where they would be welcome. A more practical explanation is that they arose during religious suppression to show a priest homes where entering to say mass was safe.

Yule. Though now used as an alternate name for Christmas, Yule was originally a German-Celtic feast at the beginning of November. After the Roman conquest, the feast became part of the winter solstice celebration and therefore was in place to become associated with Christmas.

The Yule log is probably a leftover from this winter solstice custom. A bonfire was a common feature of the celebration, just as it was at midsummer. Revelers brought in the Yule log of oak, pine, ash, or birch. In Great Britain, before the Christmas tree became part of the tradition, the Yule log played a major role in celebrations there.

Usually people kindled the Yule log on Christmas Eve with remnants of the previous year's log. According to some, the log should burn the entire twelve days of Christmas. Others state only it must be lit daily until Twelfth Night. Once Christmas was over, each family removed whatever remained of the log, keeping it under a bed as protection against fire and thunder.

Mistletoe. As one of the plants most clearly connected to pagan customs, the druids revered mistletoe. The Druids considered mistletoe to represent pure spirit because it never touched the earth.

People often gathered mistletoe to celebrate the winter solstice and burned it on the altar in sacrifice. Druids gathered it by cutting it with a golden knife or sickle and caught it in a clean white cloth. They regarded mistletoe as a symbol of future hope and peace.

Perhaps the modern custom of kissing under the mistletoe came from a custom of that time. Whenever enemies met under the mistletoe, they would drop their weapons and embrace one another.

According to old custom, there is etiquette to kissing under the mistletoe. Each time a boy kisses a girl under the mistletoe, he must remove a single berry from the plant. When all berries are gone, the mistletoe loses its spell and no more kisses are available.

The church never sanctioned the use of mistletoe because of its origin. Even now mistletoe is seldom used to decorate churches.

Holly, ivy, and other Christmas greenery. Using evergreens seems to be a pre-Christian tradition. People used green wreaths in magical rites to ensure the return of vegetation in the spring. They considered evergreens magical because they stayed green when other vegetation lost its leaves.

Decorating Christian homes with greenery became widespread after A.D. 313, though celebrants took care to choose greens that wouldn't make a pagan statement.

People adopted holly as a Christian symbol and used it in churches when mistletoe wasn't allowed. An evergreen, holly was included with other evergreens as being considered magical, but it wasn't singled out as especially sacred.

Holly reminded Christians of Jesus' crown of thorns. One legend even states that His crown was made of holly, and the previously white berries turned red when His blood touched them. Either way, the red berries remind Christians of His blood shed for us. Another legend says that the burning bush Moses saw in the wilderness was a holly tree.

Holly became the focus of superstition during the Middle Ages. In England, people believed it had power to give protection from witches. In Germany, worshippers brought home a branch of holly from church Christmas decorations as protection from thunder and lightening. These beliefs, however, grew out of Christian—rather than pagan—custom.

Ivy had been a symbol of the Roman god Bacchus and by extension of unrestrained drinking and eating. Its mythological associations kept it from becoming a major part of Christmas decorations.

Ivy did manage to creep into Christmas through the folk carol, "The Holly and the Ivy" which points to a once commonly-held belief that holly brought good luck to men and ivy to women.

The first plant used in Christmas decorations, the laurel—or bay—now seldom appears. Early Christians in Rome adorned their homes with laurel to celebrate victory over sin and death as signified by Jesus' birth. In the Roman world, laurel had been a symbol of triumph that translated well into Christian custom.

Candy canes. Recently, the story of the candy cane has become quite popular. Supposedly, a candy maker designed the candy cane to tell the Christmas story. He made the cane white as a reminder of Jesus' purity, and added peppermint flavor for the spices the wise men brought. The crook shape reminds us of the shepherds who were the first to hear of the newborn King and of He who is the Good Shepherd. Upside down, it makes a J, the first letter of Jesus' name. The red stripes were a reminder that He died for us.

The candy cane got its start many years ago when a choirmaster in Cologne, Germany handed out sticks of hard sugar candy to restless youngsters at a living Nativity in the Cathedral. In honor of the occasion, he had the candy maker bend the sticks into a shepherd's crook. The tradition spread and candy canes, often decorated with red roses, became traditional gifts accompanying Nativity plays. The tradition came to America with German settlers. For years, candy canes had to be made by hand. Then Fr. Gregory Keller, a Catholic priest, invented a machine to automate the production of candy canes in the 1950s, which allowed the company to produce larger numbers easily and then ship nationwide.

Chrismons. Chrismons are a new addition to Christmas traditions. The first Chrismon tree appeared in the nave of Ascension Lutheran Church in Danville, Virginia in 1957. The idea came from a desire to make the traditional Christmas tree—considered by many as out of place in church—more meaningful for Christians. The word *chrismon* comes from a combination of the words **Chris**t and **Mon**ogram.

A Chrismon, then, is an ornament that is a monogram for Christ. Over time, makers have applied the term to other symbols—not just initials—but all point directly to Jesus. You can make ornaments with a variety of different materials, but all should be a combination of gold and white. White is the liturgical color for Christmas and stands for the Lord's purity and perfection. Gold is traditionally used for majesty and glory. White lights on the tree carry out the theme and also point to Jesus as Light of the world. A book on church symbols provides many more options.

Poinsettias. With its red and green foliage, the poinsettia is a perfect symbol for Christmas. People in Mexico call it the "flower of the holy night."

Legend tells of a village with a custom of placing gifts for the Christ child before the crèche in the church on Christmas

Eve. A small boy with nothing to give knelt to pray in the snow outside. When he rose, a beautiful plant with scarlet leaves grew where he knelt. He presented it as his gift for the Christ child. Joel R. Poinsett, the first American minister to Mexico introduced the poinsettia to America and gave it his name.

Xmas. Probably one of the most misunderstood customs is abbreviating Christmas by writing Xmas. Some seem to feel that in doing so, people are attempting to "x-out" Christ.

Actually, Xmas is a true abbreviation of the word *Christmas.* In Greek, the first letter of Christ's name is *chi,* which is written in Greek as X. The equivalent to Xmas, transliterated completely into English, would be Chimas or C'mas, abbreviating Christ's name rather than writing out the word. The *Oxford English Dictionary* mentions a longer version, *X'temmas,* dating from 1551. Another source indicated that the abbreviation might have been used as early as the twelfth century.

Nativity scenes. When you think of a nativity scene or crèche, you usually think of figurines, not paintings. Christians began illustrating the Nativity not long after it happened.

The first was a wall decoration from about A.D. 380, found in the burial chamber of a Christian family in St. Sebastian's Catacombs in Rome. Through the years, artists have shown the nativity in all forms of artwork, which gradually led to the familiar manger scenes in many homes and churches today.

In A.D. 440, Pope Sixtus III dedicated a chapel in the Church of Santa Maria Maggiore with a replica of the manger in Bethlehem. Most likely, worshippers held the first midnight Christmas mass there.

In the eighth century, Gregory III placed a statue of Mary

and Jesus beside the manger. This foreshadowed the elaborate scenes to come. Over the years, the manger became highly decorated, more like a jeweled box, and served mainly as a centerpiece for the nativity story. By the year 1000, mangers appeared in most churches at Christmas.

In the thirteenth century, Arnolfo di Cambio sculpted the first nativity scene with freestanding figures for the chapel in the Church of Santa Maria Maggiore. By this time, devotion to Jesus as a baby was so strong in Rome that other churches set up replicas of the manger, too.

Early depictions of the manger weren't realistic. They frequently showed an altar-like table with the baby lying on it. As early as the fourth century, artists included the ox and donkey to identify the scene, even though Scripture doesn't say they were present at the first Christmas. Isaiah 1:3 states "The ox knows his master, the donkey his owner's manger, but Israel does not know, my people do not understand."

People generally interpreted this as a Messianic prophecy. Over time, the animals came to have symbolic meaning. The ox represented the Jews, who were under the yoke of the law, while the donkey represented the heathen.

Some early artists painted Jesus lying on sheaves of wheat instead of straw in the manger. Using wheat instead of straw linked the Eucharist, made of wheat, with the body of the Savior.

Pictures led in time to drama. In the tenth century, the monks of St. Gaul led the growth of new musical forms that lent themselves well to drama. The first church dramas showed the visit of the women to the tomb of Christ. The visit of the shepherds to the manger soon followed.

The first Nativity play was *Officium Pastorum*, the Office of the Shepherds. During the play, a veiled picture of Mary with

Jesus or veiled figures sat on the altar. Two groups of clerics represented the shepherds and the two midwives.

The midwives may seem slightly out of place. They were popular characters in early dramas and art. They came from an apocryphal book, the *Protoevangelium of James*. Scholars never considered the book historically accurate, but it was popular, and many elements became part of how people saw the Nativity.

As the plays developed in different areas, they began to become more elaborate. The plays reached their full development in the eleventh century. Over time they began to merge. The clergy preferred the Magi scenes to shepherd scenes, so when the two plays merged, the Magi took precedence. Perhaps this explains why the Magi began appearing at the manger, despite the fact that most scholars believe they didn't actually visit until as much as two years later.

As the plays grew larger, people began building elaborate sets within the church for the plays. Recall that churches didn't have pews at this time, so there was plenty of room.

They also began using puppets for some characters. In some cases, the puppets performed the entire play. In others, the puppets performed alongside actors. The alternative name for puppet, *marionette*, may come from this tradition. The word means "little Mary" and may come from using puppets for the Virgin Mary at nativity plays and the three Marys at the tomb in Easter plays.

In 1223, St. Francis of Assisi created the first living nativity scene. Previous displays had been set up inside the church, but St. Francis chose to place his outside. The scenes inside the church used carved figures, while St. Francis used people and animals. St. Francis had visited Bethlehem before he set up his scene, so it may have been motivated by his memories of the actual place. Later, those following in his footsteps, the Franciscans, popularized the idea over a larger area. Within a hundred years, every church was expected to have a nativity scene at Christmas.

The combination of puppets and drama eventually led to the first small nativity scenes. It was only a small step from puppets to poseable figures representing the Nativity.

The crèche began in Naples. The word crèche is French, and may come from the village of Greccio (pronounced Grecho) where St. Francis set up his first crèche. The miniature scenes made of wood or clay began as replicas of the Holy Land. Soon, however, artisans were making entire villages in miniature that looked more like their own communities than Bethlehem.

Craftsmen created the first scenes for churches or monasteries. The first in a private home belonged to Constanza Piccolomini di Aragona, Duchess of Amalf. Her elaborate scene had 167 figures and was probably made before 1567. The craft continued to grow until at the beginning of the eighteenth century, the Christmas crib, or *presepio* in Italian, had developed into a popular art in Naples.

Around 1800, the tradition spread to the Provence region of France when a group of Italian peddlers from Naples appeared in the streets of Marseilles selling small plaster figures. The *santi belli* included a variety of figures besides the Holy Family, as was popular in Naples. Local artisans liked the figures and began making similar ones called *santon* using pottery clay.

About this time Antoine Maurel wrote a mystery play called "Pastorale" that dramatized how the shepherds learned of

Jesus' birth and led the entire village—including other shepherds they met on the way—to bring gifts and greetings to the Christ Child. The *santon* makers then added shepherds in a variety of poses to their figures for the crèche.

In Germany, carved wooden figures became popular. Then, in the late eighteenth century, printers in Augsburg began making heavy paper or cardboard cutouts with manger figures. People could buy the cutouts in color or in black and white and color them by hand. Peddlers even sold a choice of one hundred different paper figures door-to-door during Advent.

In England a different tradition arose. There, families baked a mince pie in the shape of a manger. Often, they placed a figure of the Christ Child in the slight depression on the top. Once served, the pie became an object of devotion as well as part of the meal. When they removed the figure, children gleefully ate the "manger."

The tradition continued until the rise of Puritan influence. They protested mince pies as idolatry and superstition. The Catholics and Anglicans, on the other side, rose to their defense. Eventually, whether or not someone ate mince pie became a test of orthodoxy. When the Puritans took power, they passed legislation prohibiting mince pie as "idolatrie in crust."

Moravians introduced the crèche to America from Germany in the mid-1700s. They called their nativity scene a *putz* from the German word putzen (or decorate). By the 1890s, American stores sold plaster and lead nativity figures as well as the materials needed to make crèches.

The nativity play is an American version of the old mystery plays. Unlike the old mystery plays, they stick close to

Scripture. Children at Holy Trinity Church in Boston, Massachusetts, performed the first nativity play in America during the Christmas season of 1851. The costumed children carried bundles of food, cloth, and other gifts to a crib on the altar, singing Christmas carols as they came.

At the altar a priest received the gifts, which were then distributed to the poor. The simple pageant attracted so much attention that it had to be repeated twice during Christmas week, at the request of Catholics and Protestants alike. The custom spread quickly across the country.

Santa Claus. Santa Claus has his beginning in St. Nicholas, bishop of Myra. His change into Santa Claus began with the German Reformation. The German pronunciation of *Christkindl* (both i's are short) became anglicized as "Kriss Kringle," Santa's other name.

If not for several different pieces of literature, Santa might have remained more a religious than a secular figure. Or at least, he might have been a regional part of Christmas rather than a general one. In 1809, Washington Irving continually mentioned St. Nicholas in his *Diedrich Knickerbocker's History of New York from the Beginning of the World to the End of the Dutch Dynasty.* This introduced St. Nicholas to many that had never heard of him. Secularization also began, since Irving presented him as a pipe-smoking Dutchman rather than as a bishop.

The process continued with the publication of Clement Clark Moore's poem "A Visit from St. Nicholas." Moore was of Dutch ancestry himself. He later said that he had modeled his version of St. Nick on a "portly rubicund Dutchman" who had lived near his father's home, though he borrowed many elements from Irving's work. He also added touches of his own.

Moore titled the poem "A Visit from St. Nicholas," but it was Santa who emerged.

Moore first shared the poem with his children on December 23, 1822. He didn't want to publish it, as he felt it would damage his reputation as a serious scholar. A friend of the family who had read the poem sent a copy of it to *The Troy Sentinel,* where it was published on December 23, 1823. Moore didn't claim the poem as his until 1844, when he finally included it in a collection of his works.

Two books published in 1842 and 1845, respectively, *Kriss Kringle's Book* and *Kriss Kringle's Christmas Tree,* both helped spread Santa's popularity and completed the merge of the Christkindl with Santa Claus. *Kriss Kringle's Christmas Tree* holds another distinction. The illustration on the title page may show Santa Claus and the Christmas tree together for the first time in this country. The tree bears little resemblance to our Christmas tree. It has regular leaves rather than needles. Santa hung toys from his pack on the tree instead of putting them under it.

Santa's elves appeared as early as 1856. Louisa May Alcott wrote, but didn't publish, a book titled *Christmas Elves.* Elves were a natural addition to a fairy-tale-like Santa. An engraving in *Godey's Lady's Book* from 1873 shows the elves in Santa's workshop. The elves got additional recognition in 1876, when Edward Eggleston wrote *The House of Santa Claus, a Christmas Fairy Show for Sunday Schools.*

Thomas Nast, editorial cartoonist at Harper's Weekly popularized the Santa Claus story with his drawings. His first illustration of Santa Claus appeared in 1862. At this time, Moore's poem was already in existence, and he probably knew it. Some elements in his illustrations came from Moore's poem, but others are original.

He added Santa's home at the North Pole and established that Santa uses a telescope to see whether children are good or bad. He also showed Santa's book recording good and bad children, and gave glimpses of Santa's home life. Nast's grandson later claimed that he chose the North Pole for Santa's home because it was equidistant from most countries in the Northern Hemisphere.

Santa Claus, as we know him today, also contains many elements of the Norse god, Thor, whom artists showed as a large, elderly man with a long white beard. People considered him a cheerful and friendly god who always helped them. According to legend, Thor lived in the "North-land" where he had his palace among icebergs.

Thor's "element" was fire and his color was red. The fireplace was especially sacred to him and many stories said he came down the chimney into the fire. These sound like Santa Claus. Moore and Nast may have used these elements of Norse mythology to shape their visions of Santa Claus.

Another source gave a different story of why Santa comes down the chimney. Hertha or Bertha was a Norse goddess of domesticity and the home. People decorated houses with fir and evergreens during the winter solstice to welcome her coming.

When the family gathered to eat, they built an altar of flat stones and laid a fire of fir boughs. Hertha descended through the smoke to bless the home. Santa's habit of coming down the chimney instead of entering through the door may be the only survival of this tradition.

Children began writing letters to Santa as early as 1874. The idea apparently spread quickly. Children flooded the post office with letters by the 1890s.

The first of the familiar department store Santas appeared in 1890. James Edgar, a storeowner in Brockton, Massachusetts, had tried a variety of costumes to get parents to bring children in the store. A clown, various war heroes, and Uncle Sam met with limited success. Dressing as Santa brought children flocking into the store. Word of the response to Santa spread and now you can find Santa at malls across America.

Mrs. Claus made her debut in 1899 in a book titled *Goody Santa Claus on a Sleigh Ride*. The book was one of thirty-two written by Katharine Lee Bates, better known as the composer of *America the Beautiful*. Goody was a contraction of "Good Wife," an early New England term used instead of Mrs.

No one is sure when children began leaving food for Santa Claus. In 1908, the *New York Tribune* told its readers how children in one family left out a lunch for Santa. They had reasoned that he would be tired after all his hard work. The children set the table, ground coffee, and left out covered sandwiches and cake. The next morning the food had vanished and they found a note pinned to the Christmas tree thanking them for their kindness.

At one time, children also left out carrots or hay for Santa's reindeer. Children in the country, who knew what animals needed, left piles of salt on their windowsills for them. The next morning, a smudged window and no salt announced Santa and his reindeer's arrival during the night.

A marketing campaign made Santa Claus the figure we know today. In 1930, Coca-Cola adopted him as their trademark for a time, and artist Haddon Sundbloom's portrayal of him as a plump, jolly, red-cheeked man became the popular image.

The only major piece left to be added to the Santa myth was

a special reindeer named Rudolph. A publication called *The Children's Friend* first mentioned Santa's reindeer in 1821: "Old Santa Claus with much delight, His reindeer drives this frosty night." Moore gave all the reindeer names in his poem.

Robert May added Rudolph the Red Nosed Reindeer to the group in 1939. A copywriter for Montgomery Ward, May wrote the story as a giveaway for the department store Santas. During the initial run in 1939, the store gave away 2.4 million copies.

When Ward's used the story again in 1946, they gave away an additional 3.6 million. After the second printing, Ward's returned the copyright to May. He eventually found a publisher for the story and sold 100,000 copies the first year. Then, in 1949, May and his brother-in-law, Johnny Marks turned Rudolph into a song. Gene Autry recorded the new song, and Rudolph became a permanent part of the Santa story.

Christmas Music

Carols are one of the most familiar and joyful parts of Christmas. Most people consider all Christmas songs to be Christmas carols. Technically speaking, the older ballads with no known composer are the only true carols. The other songs are hymns. They have specific composers and are more elaborate musically.

Early Latin hymns. Latin hymns for church worship became the first Christmas music. We have examples as old as the fourth century. Modern listeners would find them stiff and formal, as they focused more on the theological part of Christmas. Writers made no attempt to imagine the stable or see Jesus as a real baby. They wanted to reinforce the spiritual, not human, parts of Christmas.

Macaronic carols. Though secular carols existed earlier, the first religious carols date back to the late thirteenth or the fourteenth century. The word *carol* originally referred to a dance, usually a ring dance, often with words that indicated actions. People used secular carols for joyful, exuberant celebrations.

This joy began to spill over into the popular culture's celebration of Christmas. Composers used common language instead of Latin. Also, they began focusing on the human side of the Nativity: the emotions of the participants or the lowly surroundings.

Early macaronic carols provided a bridge between the church Latin hymns and popular music. Carol writers inserted fragments of Latin texts into lyrics written in their own language. Sometimes the Latin was only a word or two, while in other carols entire lines in Latin alternated with everyday speech.

After the macaronic carols, most of the later English carols were ballads. People first heard and sang the traditional carols from the fifteenth to the eighteenth centuries.

St. Francis and the carols. People often credit St. Francis of Assisi with popularizing or even creating Christmas carols. Accounts of the first crèche say that he burst into joyful song when he saw the people's response. Carol singing became part of later crèche celebrations throughout Italy.

One of his disciples, Jacopone di Todi, wrote the first Christmas songs in Italian. He and other Franciscans wanted to help people see the human aspects of the gospel while not forgetting the divine.

Some of the Italian carols shaped how people view the Nativity today. Many nativity scenes show the Baby Jesus lying nearly naked on the hay with His arms stretched out. The idea grew out of the Italian emphasis on the poverty and simplicity of His birth.

German carols. Later in the fourteenth century, Germany was developing carols, partially due to Eckhart of Strasburg's preaching. A Dominican, he focused on the Divine Birth in the soul of a believer. This led to a greater focus on the physical birth of Jesus at Christmas.

Following the pattern of other carols, German carols focused more on the human emotions in the Nativity. *Hirtenlieder*—or shepherd songs—were particularly popular. The rural people identified with the shepherds of Bethlehem and tried to share their emotions at the first Christmas. Refrains often imitated shepherds' instruments.

Another German carol was the companion carol. The singer in this type of carol imagined himself accompanying the shepherds or others to visit Baby Jesus. Composers wrote in local dialects to add familiarity to the song.

Personal religion—rather than theological doctrine—is stronger in German music than in any other. The German Reformation gave rise to some of the best Christmas hymns. Unlike the English Reformation, the German Reformation didn't restrict celebrating Christmas. Martin Luther wrote some of the German hymns and Paul Gerhardt, a seventeenth-century Berlin pastor, wrote others.

They began to blur the line between hymns and carols because they believed in using popular melodies for their messages. In all of his hymn writing, not just Christmas hymns,

Luther believed in using common language to make ideas accessible to anyone.

One of Luther's best-known hymns is not actually written by him. People often refer to "Away in a Manger" as "Luther's Cradle Hymn" but he wrote neither words nor music. The familiar English text is American, probably written by German Lutherans in Pennsylvania. The poem first appeared in print in Philadelphia in 1885.

The second part in the first stanza of Luther's hymn *Vom Himmel Kam der Engel Schar* may have inspired the song. This line, in English, reads "Away there in the manger a little Infant lies." The similarity to Luther's hymn and the fact that a Lutheran wrote it may have resulted in confusion.

French Noels. French carols developed about the same time as the English carols. The main difference, other than the language, is that the French Noel was specifically written for Christmas. Carolers repeated the word *noel* as part of the refrain. The familiar tune to "O Come, O Come, Emmanuel" is from a fifteenth century French Noel.

Where the French *noel* came from as a word for Christmas is uncertain. It may have its roots in the Latin *natalis* or "birthday." The other possibility is from the old English word *nowell*, which means "news." In carols, *noel* is often used in the sense of bringing news, as in "The First Noel." Both may be correct. The two words *noel* and *nowell* had different origins, but they came to mean the same thing because people pronounced them the same.

Ballad carols. A ballad is a simple poem telling a popular story in short stanzas. Ballad carols can be divided into different types.

Many are nativity ballads. They tell the story of Jesus' birth, often from different points of view. The familiar "God Rest Ye Merry, Gentlemen" is a nativity ballad written from the point of view of the shepherds who are telling the Good News.

Legendary or mystery carols are another group of ballads. These focus on different legends surrounding the Nativity. Some may go back to apocryphal stories retold in song.

Lullabies in which the writer imagines words Mary might have sung while cradling her baby are another type of ballad carol. Mary, of course, is well represented in carols. Before the Reformation, a large body of *Marienlieder* songs became popular. These songs focused on Mary rather than on her son. After the Reformation, people adapted many of these to the new focus on Jesus by substituting His name for Mary's name.

Prayer carols are quite similar to lullabies. In these, the singer addresses Jesus directly with wonder, devotion, and admiration.

People sang doctrinal carols about other parts of the Redemption at other seasons. Some of these were sung at Christmas as well. It became common to focus on Christ's entire life, not just His birth during the Christmas season.

Number carols are an unusual type of ballad carols. Examples are "The Seven Joys of Mary" and "The Twelve Days of Christmas." The children's song "This Old Man" is a secular number carol.

The last two types of ballad carols are secular rather than sacred, but are still a part of our celebration. The first are wassail carols such as "Here We Come a Caroling." The original wording, sometimes still heard today, was "Here We Come a Wassailing." These were purely fun songs used during feudal days when vassals expected their masters to share food and drink with them at Christmas.

The final type is the folklore carol. These deal with traditional elements of the Christmas celebration that aren't necessarily Christian. "The Holly and the Ivy" is a folklore carol reflecting traditions associated with the two plants. Like other early carols, the symbolism may go back to pre-Christian traditions.

The medieval mystery plays gave carols an additional boost. Christmas was a popular theme for the various plays. As the plays developed, various composers wrote more and more music to go along with them.

Carols fell out of favor in England after 1647, and the Puritan Commonwealth. The new government forbade carols and mystery plays along with all other parts of the Christmas celebration. When the monarchy was restored, carols gradually regained favor, though not to the same level as before.

Christmas hymns. The eighteenth century saw the rise of Christmas hymns. With the decline of carols, new music needed to fill the gap. Some composers of the first hymns went back to earlier poems to find lyrics for new music. Therefore, even though the hymn is considered to be eighteenth-century, some lyrics are older.

Isaac Watts' hymnbooks were the first to receive wide circulation. Of his, the most important was *Hymns and Spiritual Songs*, published in 1707. Others followed.

English carols received a rebirth in the nineteenth century. People began making efforts to find and preserve old carols before they died out. In 1833, William Sandys released *Selection of Christmas Carols, Ancient and Modern*. J.M. Neale's *Carols for Christmastide* followed in 1852.

The process of recording and publishing carols brought them back instead. In combination with a new emphasis on

Christmas and the popularization of the Christmas tree and Christmas cards, carols made a comeback.

The confusion between hymns and carols is fairly recent. The first hymnbook to include both may have been the *Oxford Hymn Book* of 1908. *Congregational Hymnary* had eleven carols separate from the hymns in 1916.

Christmas music in America. The older hymns and carols are still favorites today. As with other traditions, Christmas music in America is a blend from various countries. We have inherited some of the best, but we have added our own touches.

A missionary to the Huron Indians, John de Brébeuf, wrote the first American carol. He worked among the Hurons until 1626, when the Iroquois captured and killed him. Appropriately for a carol, he wrote it in the Huron language and modeled it after a sixteenth-century French folk song. The Hurons preserved *Jesous Ahatonnia* (Jesus is Born) until a later missionary could write it down.

America has added popular Christmas hymns to the standard list. During the nineteenth century, revival and the growth of Christmas customs spurred new music. Familiar American Christmas hymns include "It Came Upon the Midnight Clear" written in 1876, by Edmund H. Sears.

Phillips Brooks wrote "O Little Town of Bethlehem" after a visit to Israel where he visited the site of the Nativity. The organist of Holy Trinity Church in Philadelphia, where Brooks was then rector, wrote the tune in 1865. Children in the Sunday school sang the hymn for the first time on Christmas 1868.

Secular Christmas music developed at the same time. John Pierpont wrote "Jingle Bells" in 1856. In 1863, *Godey's Lady's*

Book announced the forthcoming release of new music for the season.

As musical styles changed in America, Christmas music has changed along with them. "Santa Claus is Coming to Town" made an appearance in 1934. "'Twas the Night Before Christmas" came out in the 1930s. Both foreshadowed the coming boom in secular Christmas music.

Though composers had written and released new Christmas music before, 1942 heralded the real birth of secular Christmas music in America when "White Christmas," sung by Bing Crosby in *Holiday Inn*, won an Oscar. Since then people have bought over thirty million copies of the song, and artists from all genres have recorded it.

The popularity of "White Christmas" set the standard for much of the new Christmas music. Home and nostalgia became familiar themes for most new releases. World War II may have been a factor as homesick GIs remembered Christmases past.

The trend continued in 1944 when Judy Garland sang "Have Yourself a Merry Little Christmas" in *Meet Me in St. Louis*. Every year thereafter to the end of the decade, saw the addition of a song now considered part of the accepted list of Christmas songs. In 1945, "Let It Snow, Let It Snow, Let It Snow!" joined the group, while in 1946, the warm and cozy "The Christmas Song (Chestnuts Roasting on an Open Fire)" debuted.

"Here Comes Santa Claus" in 1947 did more than add a new song to the list. Both it and the later "Rudolph the Red-Nosed Reindeer" were among the first to use pictures on the record sleeve as a marketing tool. Shrewd producers thought a cartoon picture of Santa on the cover would make a child beg for the record, resulting in added sales for the company.

Before long, color covers were a regular part of the music industry.

Novelty songs began appearing at the end of the 1940s and into the 1950s. While some of the earlier songs might be considered novelties, composers intended them for children. The newer novelty songs amused an adult audience. "All I Want for Christmas (Is My Two Front Teeth)" was the first in 1948.

"Rudolph the Red-Nosed Reindeer" moved from children's book to song in 1949. Not only did it contribute to a new marketing strategy it holds a dubious distinction as setting a new trend for Christmas as a marketing vehicle. "Rudolph" owed its entire existence to marketing, from the first book to the song and later, TV special.

In 1950 came "Frosty the Snow Man." The television special came much later, in 1969. Novelty still reigned with "I Saw Mommy Kissing Santa Claus" in 1952 and "Nuttin' for Christmas" in 1955. "Sweet Little Jesus Boy" also came out in 1955, showing that composers hadn't completely forgotten the sacred.

"Mary's Boy Child" arrived in 1956, while 1957 featured the arrival of "Jingle Bell Rock." The flood of music began to slow toward the end of the 1950s. Only a few more songs became part of the music usually heard at Christmas.

In 1958, "The Little Drummer Boy" took its place as a Christmas icon. Like others, the song eventually became a TV special, in 1968 and 1976. A totally different song, "Rockin' Around the Christmas Tree" was released in 1958 as well. Finally, "Winter Wonderland" entered the scene in 1964.

With the 1960s, music began to segment into different styles. Christmas music was no longer as important, and most Christmas albums featured new renditions of older music rather than completely new songs. Those featuring new music seldom reached beyond the particular style's market. Today the market waits for another new song that will break out of its genre to become the latest addition to Christmas songs in America.

The growth of Gospel and contemporary Christian music as separate styles added more titles to the list of Christmas music choices. While these haven't been added to more traditional hymnals, the newer contemporary hymnals focusing on praise and worship styles have begun to add modern Christmas music.

Even though all hymnals may not feature contemporary Christmas music, some titles are beginning to move into traditional circles. People sing "Mary Did you Know" by Mark Lowery and Buddy Greene in both traditional and progressive churches.

For contemporary Christian and gospel music lovers, most popular artists release a Christmas album. These tend to feature a mix of old and new. Older songs may be given a more contemporary setting in keeping with the artists' style. New songs specifically written for Christmas may also debut on each release.

If Christmas is your favorite time of year, you're in good company. The rich traditions of the season make it special for many. As Christians, we have the best of both worlds: rich and varied traditions set into the knowledge that God sent us a Savior. For us, the heart of the season is Immanuel: God with us.

Handling the Holidays

Christians have been asking how to handle holidays since the beginning of the Christian faith. Unfortunately, Paul wasn't inspired to write 1 and 2 Holidays outlining what Christians should celebrate and how to do so.

Because of this, holidays fall into the gray area of our faith. Unless Scripture specifically contradicts part of a celebration, it is up to us to decide how to handle these celebrations.

Paul dealt with a similar situation when he wrote about the problem of meat sacrificed to idols in 1 Corinthians. Believers were unsure whether or not Christians could eat this meat. Paul left the matter to the believer's conscience. In doing so, he also left good guidelines for deciding about current customs.

Where we often go astray in thinking about the matter is in asking whether or not we may participate in a holiday or custom. Paul makes it clear that everything is permitted for Christians, though not everything is beneficial. Based on 1 Corinthians 8-10, we must ask two questions: does it glorify God? Is it beneficial to my walk with God?

Paul also discusses the issue of the weaker believer. While a choice may not bother us, God calls us to be careful that our choices not confuse or lead astray another believer with a more tender conscience.

Since we do have this freedom, celebrations may look as different as each individual. God gives us the Holy Spirit as a guide in deciding how we understand different Scriptural guidelines. We may all make different choices and disagree with some of the choices others make.

So what are the different possibilities to handling holidays and holiday customs? They range from completely accepting and celebrating a holiday, through a modified or possibly alternative celebration, to not celebrating at all.

Centuries divide the modern customs from the original ones. If you decide that the modern customs are harmless, then you may choose to participate in a holiday. The issue in deciding is to hold each custom against the measure of Scripture. Since the definition of "beneficial" depends on your conscience, our answers will probably be quite different.

For example, after learning more about the origins of Halloween, if you no longer see the "haunted" aspect of the holiday as innocent fun, you may want to participate in a different way. Consider decorating with fall fruits and vegetables, instead of a carved Jack O'lantern. Carving a pumpkin with Christian symbols is another possibility.

At the other end of the spectrum is deciding that because of the pagan associations with a given holiday, you should not participate in the holiday at all. If after prayer and consideration you don't feel comfortable with any custom, you shouldn't participate in the holiday.

It's important for us as fellow believers to accept the choices others may make. Through the years, Christians have found many areas of division. Now, more than ever, we need to show the world the love the Lord gives us for each other, even when we disagree.

Consider your choices prayerfully. Consult the Bible for guidance. Then celebrate each holiday with a clear conscience, knowing your celebration will be pleasing to God.

Children and Holidays

While the same basic guidelines on making decisions work for both children and adults, the question of handling holidays for children is a little different. Children aren't miniature adults. They don't think like adults and don't process information like adults.

Because of this, parents have to be more careful in making decisions for their children than they do for themselves. A child's conscience may be more tender than an adult's conscience. The child doesn't yet have the "filters" adults do. Things that don't bother an adult may cause problems for a child.

Specifically, children have difficulty separating fantasy from reality and think on a concrete level. We must be careful, therefore, that we do not put the real things of God on a level with those from the fantasy world. While Santa kneeling at the manger can be a meaningful symbol for adults, a child will take both at the same level of reality.

Instead of teaching the abstract lesson that the things of the world must bow to those of God, we may have put confusion in the child's mind, as they see Santa Claus and Jesus presented on the same level of reality.

Telling him or her that one is real and one is fantasy, when both are pictured together may only add to the confusion, rather than clarifying it, especially when Santa can be found at every shopping mall.

If you're thinking that your child can understand the difference if you explain it carefully, consider this example.

As a child, I remember clearly arguing with my first grade teacher and my mother that 1-1=1. The problem wasn't my teacher's explanation of subtraction. I was caught in the physical problem on the paper and couldn't understand the concept behind it.

Because I saw two 1's written on the paper, I believed that if you covered up one of the 1's, you would still have one of them left. Therefore, 1-1=1. It's a classic example of how a child can take something simple to an adult and misunderstand it.

I don't remember when I finally understood that 1-1=0, but I remember being unconvinced by the teacher's attempt to explain that it was the same 1 when I saw two of them written down.

Children are also learning. They don't have the same background adults do, especially when it comes to the Bible. They can't balance what they see and hear with other information. Because they are not as far along in learning to know God, parents should be more cautious.

It's important that parents use holidays to teach. For young children, this will be mainly by example. What you do sets an example for your child. As children grow older, you can use holidays to teach the principles you use to make decisions about them.

Remember, too, that children are as different as adults are. God gives each of us a unique personality at the beginning. Not only do children understand differently just because they are children, each child has different sensitivities. You may come up with different answers for different children.

While you don't want to overload children with information or ask them to understand differences beyond their years, don't be shy in giving explanations. Even a holiday you do not celebrate can be a teaching opportunity.

Trying to explain holidays to children can be difficult. It

can also be hard to come up with our own alternatives to holidays if you choose not to participate in all or part of one. The following books aren't a complete list of everything available, but will provide some help.

Whatever you decide, do it to the glory of God. Holidays began as holy days, so there's no reason they can't still be holy. While people look at the outward appearance, God looks at the heart. If you approach your celebration with a desire to honor God, then whatever you do is acceptable.

Resources For Families

Barnes, Emily. *The Very Best Christmas Ever.* Eugene, Ore.: Harvest House, 1998.

Barth, Edna. *Hearts, Cupids, and Red Roses: The Story of the Valentine Symbols.* New York: Clarion Books, 2001

Barth, Edna. *Holly, Reindeer, and Colored Lights: The Story of the Christmas Symbols.* New York: Clarion Books, 2000.

Barth, Edna. *Lilies, Rabbits, and Painted Eggs: The Story of the Easter Symbols.* New York: Clarion Books, 2001.

Barth, Edna. *Shamrocks, Harps, and Shillelaghs: The Story of the St. Patrick's Day Symbols.* New York: Clarion Books, 2001.

Barth, Edna. *Turkeys, Pilgrims, and Indian Corn: The Story of the Thanksgiving Symbols.* New York: Clarion Books, 2000.

Barth, Edna. *Witches, Pumpkins, and Grinning Ghosts: The Story of the Halloween Symbols.* New York: Clarion Books, 2000.

Haidle, Helen and David. *The Candymaker's Gift: A Legend of the Candy Cane.* Tulsa, Okla.: Honor, 1996.

Haidle, Helen: *The Real Twelve Days of Christmas.* Grand Rapids, Mich.: Zondervan, 1997.

Hibbard, Ann. *Family Celebrations at Easter.* Grand Rapids, Mich.: Baker, 1994.

Hibbard, Ann. *Family Celebrations at Thanksgiving and Alternatives to Halloween.* Grand Rapids, Mich.: Baker, 1995.

Higgs, Liz Curtis. *The Parable of the Lily.* Nashville, Tenn.: Thomas Nelson, 1997.

Higgs, Liz Curtis. *The Pine Tree Parable.* Nashville, Tenn.: Thomas Nelson, 1997.

Higgs, Liz Curtis. *The Pumpkin Patch Parable.* Nashville, Tenn.: Thomas Nelson, 1995.

Higgs, Liz Curtis. *The Sunflower Parable.* Nashville, Tenn.: Thomas Nelson, 1997.

Myra, Harold. *Easter Bunny: Are You for Real?* Nashville, Tenn.: Thomas Nelson, 1998.

Myra, Harold. *Halloween: Is It for Real?* Nashville, Tenn.: Thomas Nelson, 1997.

Myra, Harold. *Santa, Are You for Real?* Nashville, Tenn.: Thomas Nelson, 1997.

Walburg, Lori. *The Legend of the Candy Cane.* Grand Rapids, Mich.: Zondervan, 1997.

Walburg, Lori. *The Legend of the Easter Egg.* Grand Rapids, Mich.: Zondervan, 1999.

Winwood, Linda Hacon. *Mommy, Why Don't We Celebrate Halloween?* Shippensburg, Pa.: Destiny Image, 1994.

Zimmerman, Martha. *Celebrating the Christian Year.* Minneapolis, Minn.: Bethany, 1994.